Lounge Music
for Easy Piano

ISBN 0-7935-9650-5

HAL•LEONARD®
CORPORATION
7777 W. BLUEMOUND RD. P.O. BOX 13819 MILWAUKEE, WI 53213

Visit Hal Leonard Online at
www.halleonard.com

Lounge Music

for Easy Piano

contents

ALFIE
Theme from the Paramount Picture ALFIE

Words by HAL DAVID
Music by BURT BACHARACH

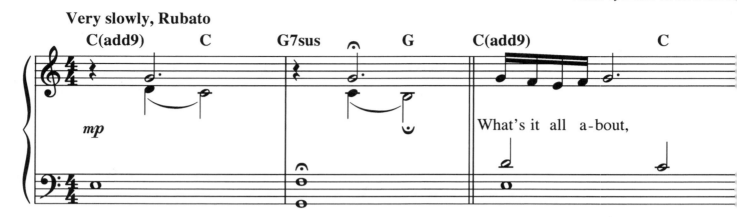

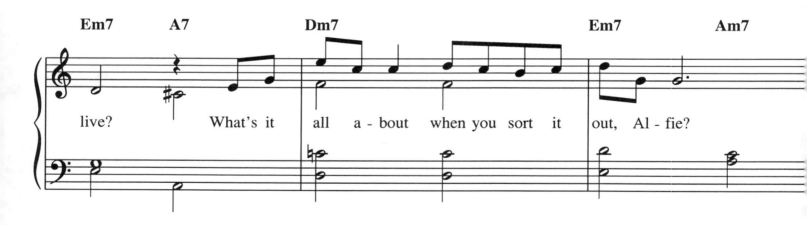

5

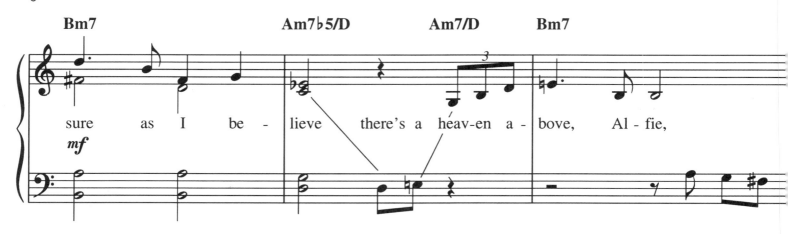

sure   as   I   be - lieve   there's a heav-en a - bove,   Al - fie,

I   know   there's some-thing much   more,   some-thing e - ven

non - be - liev - ers   can   be - lieve in.   I be-lieve in love,

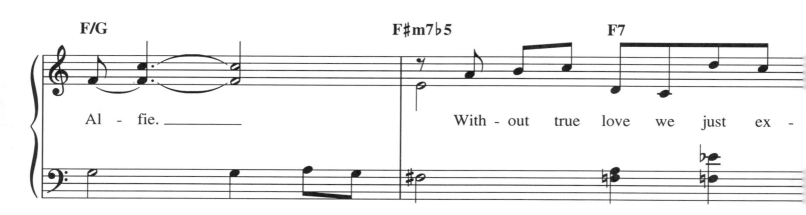

Al - fie. _____   With - out true love we just ex -

BÉSAME MUCHO
(Kiss Me Much)

Music and Spanish Words by CONSUELO VELAZQUEZ
English Words by SUNNY SKYLAR

Be - sa - me ____ be - sa - me mu - cho. ____

Each time I cling to your kiss I hear mu - sic di -

vine. Be -

- sa - me mu - cho. ____

Dm **Bb7** **A7**

Hold me, my dar - ling, and say that you'll al - ways be

Dm **Gm6**

mine. ____ This joy is some-thing new,

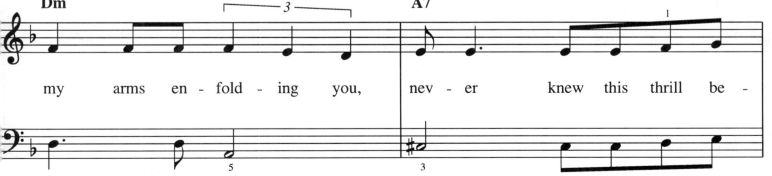

Dm **A7**

my arms en - fold - ing you, nev - er knew this thrill be -

fore. Who ev - er thought I'd be hold - ing you close to me,

whisp - 'ring "It's you I a - dore." Dear - est one,

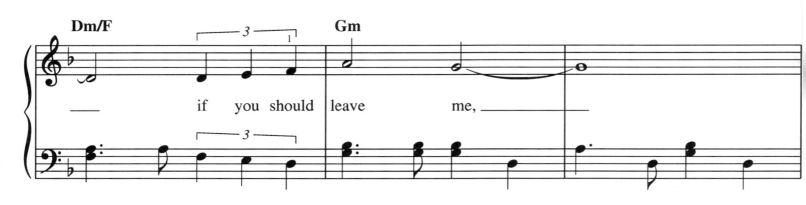

if you should leave me,

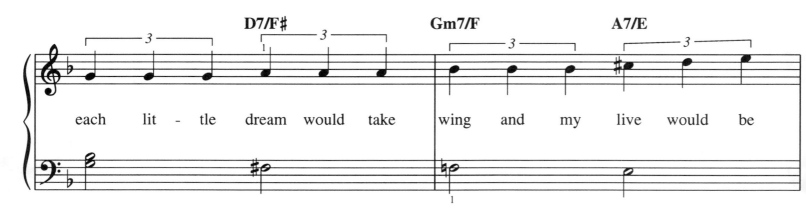

each lit - tle dream would take wing and my live would be

BEYOND THE SEA

English Lyrics by JACK LAWRENCE
Music and French Lyrics by CHARLES TRENET

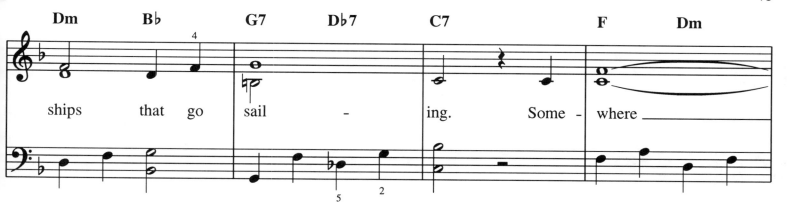

ships that go sail - ing. Some - where ___

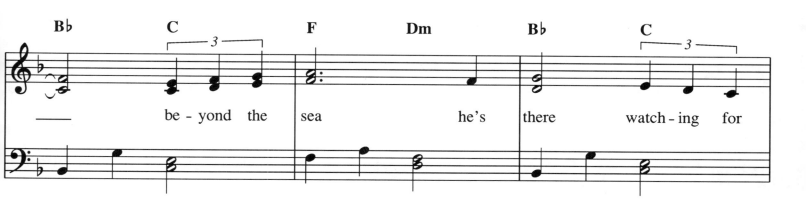

___ be - yond the sea he's there watch - ing for

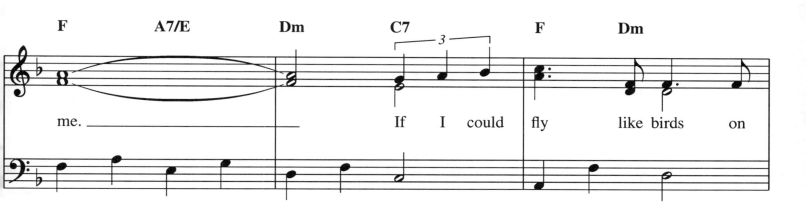

me. ___ If I could fly like birds on

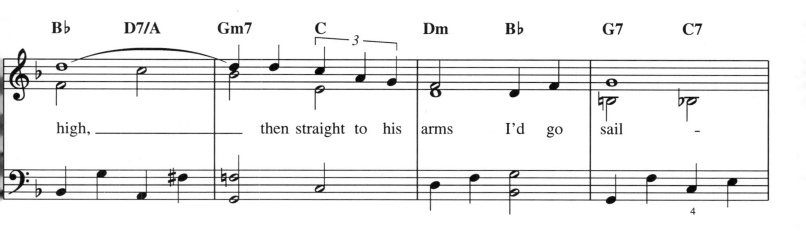

high, ___ then straight to his arms I'd go sail -

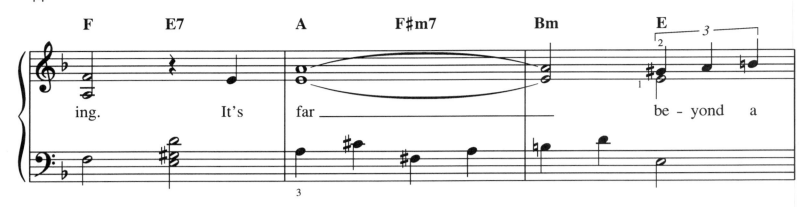

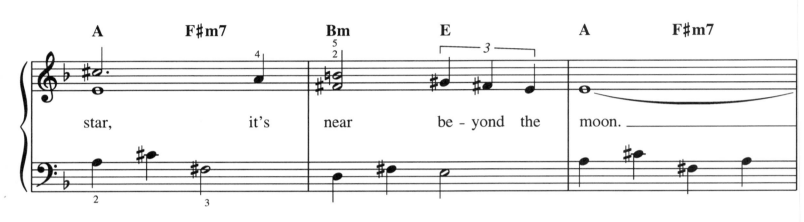

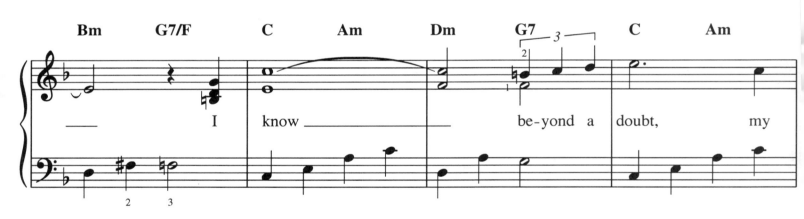

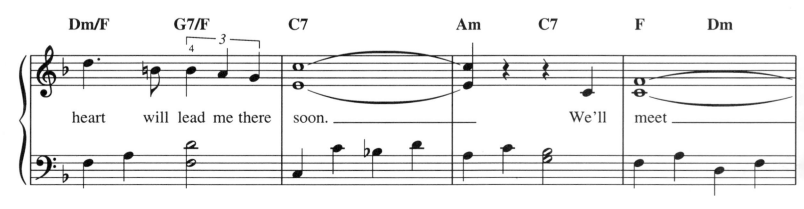

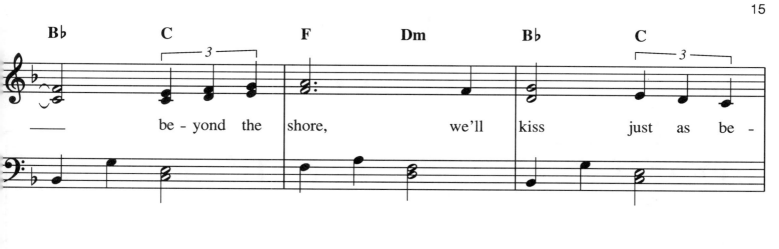

be - yond the shore, we'll kiss just as be -

fore. _____ Hap - py we'll be be - yond the

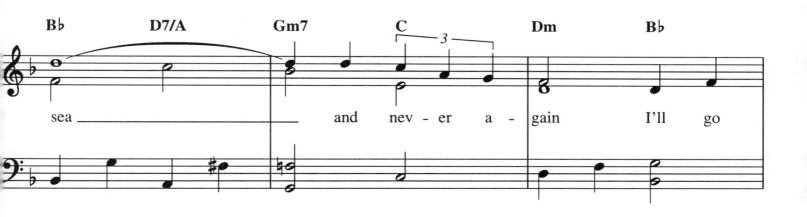

sea _____ and nev - er a - gain I'll go

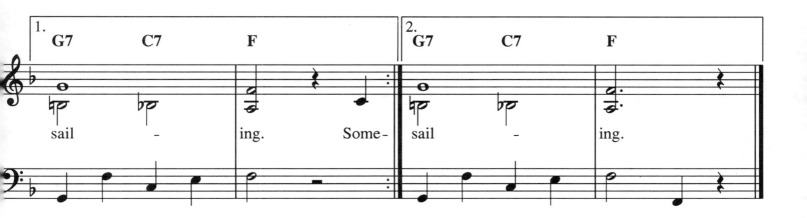

sail - ing. Some- sail - ing.

CALL ME

Words and Music by
TONY HATCH

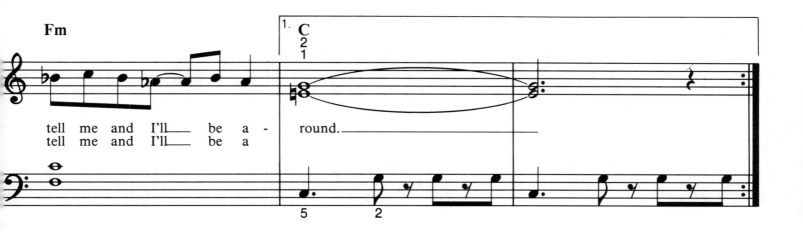

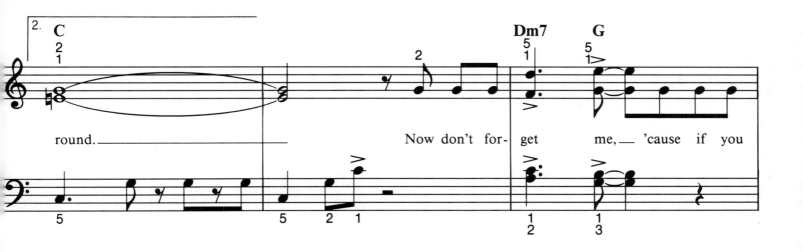

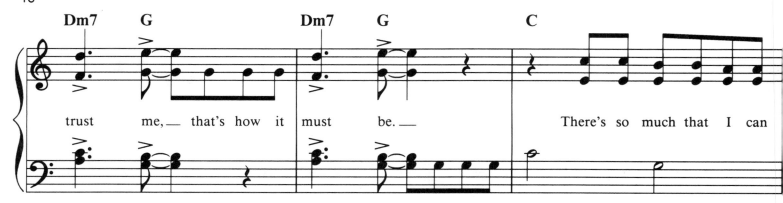

trust me,— that's how it must be.— There's so much that I can

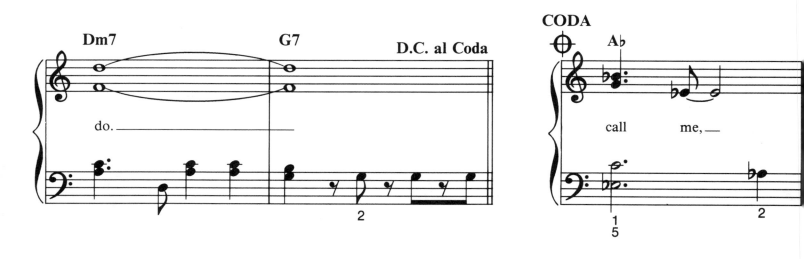

D.C. al Coda

CODA

do.—

call me,—

May - be it's late— but just call me,—

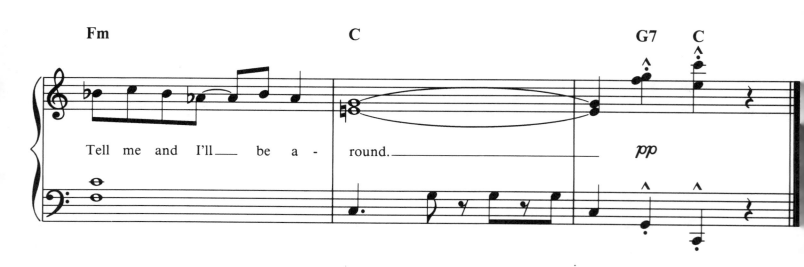

Tell me and I'll— be a - round.—

pp

BLUE VELVET

Words and Music by BERNIE WAYNE
and LEE MORRIS

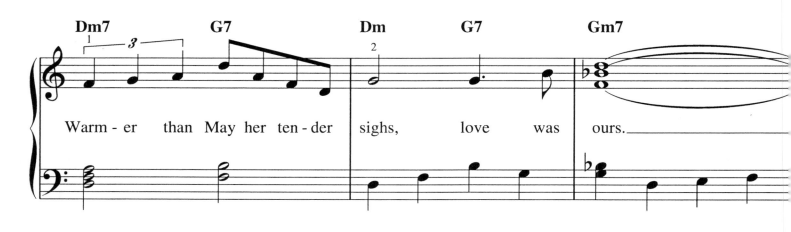

Warm - er than May her ten - der sighs, love was ours._____

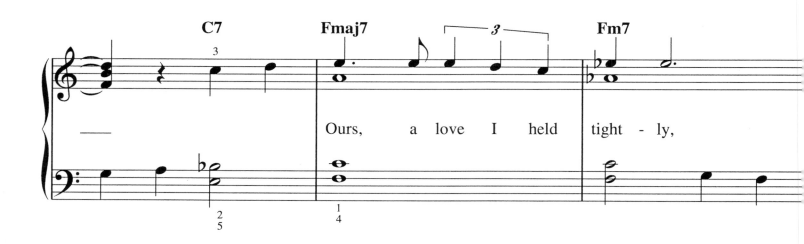

_____ Ours, a love I held tight - ly,

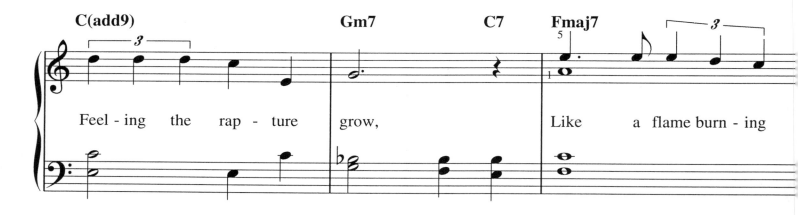

Feel - ing the rap - ture grow, Like a flame burn - ing

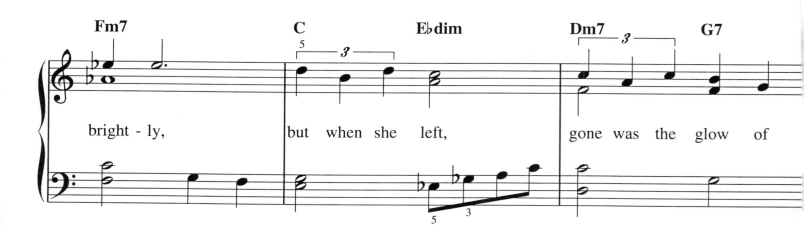

bright - ly, but when she left, gone was the glow of

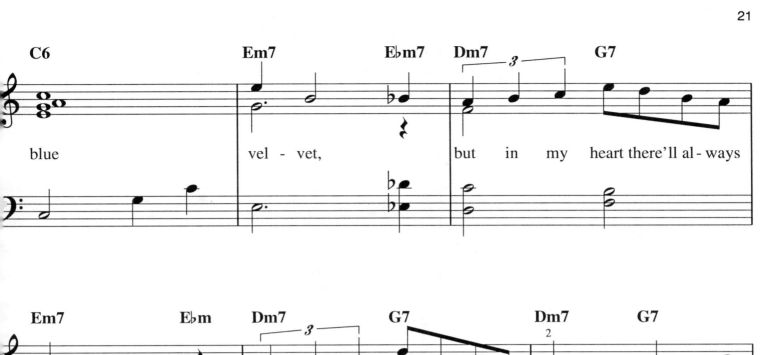

blue   vel - vet,   but   in   my   heart there'll al - ways

be,   pre - cious and   warm, a mem - o - ry   through   the

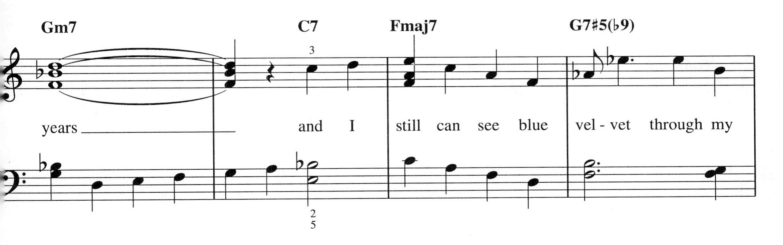

years _____   and   I   still can see blue   vel - vet   through my

tears.   She   wore   tears.   *rit.*

CALL ME IRRESPONSIBLE

from the Paramount Picture PAPA'S DELICATE CONDITION

Words by SAMMY CAHN
Music by JAMES VAN HEUSEN

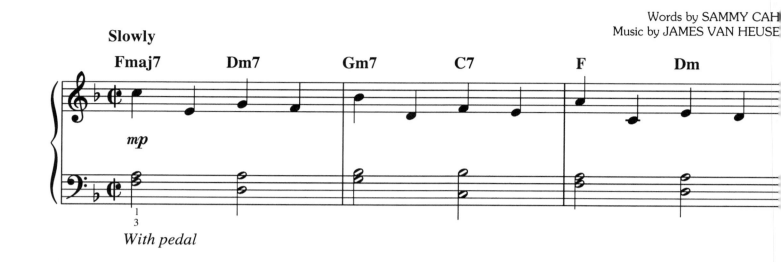

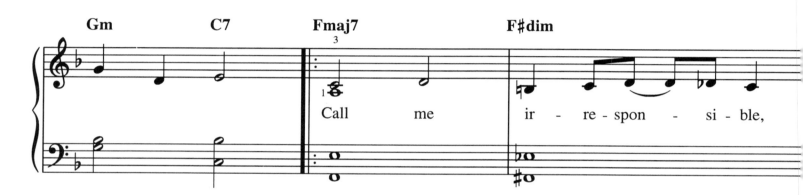

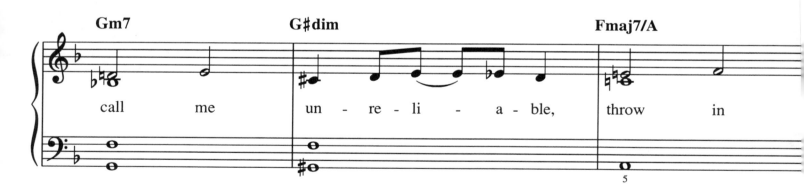

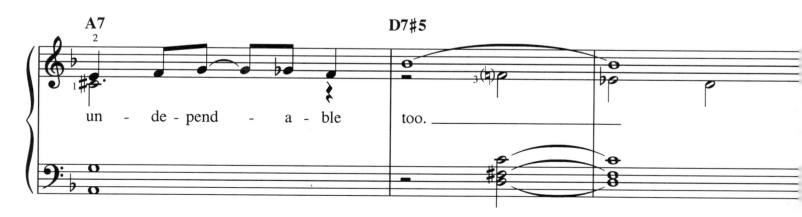

Do my fool - ish al - i - bis bore

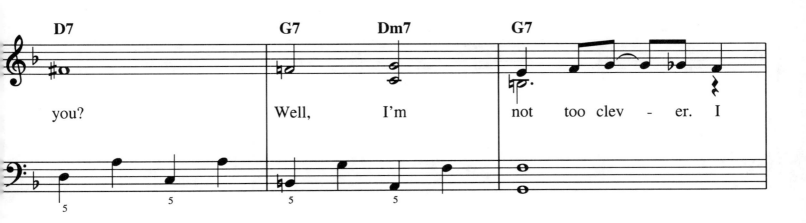

you? Well, I'm not too clev - er. I

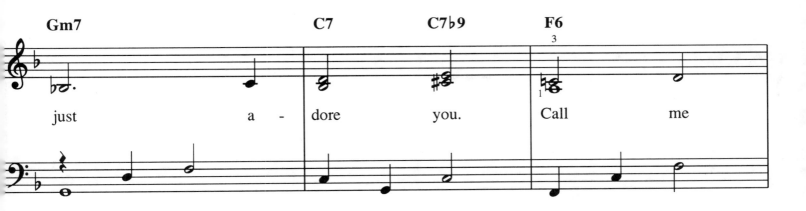

just a - dore you. Call me

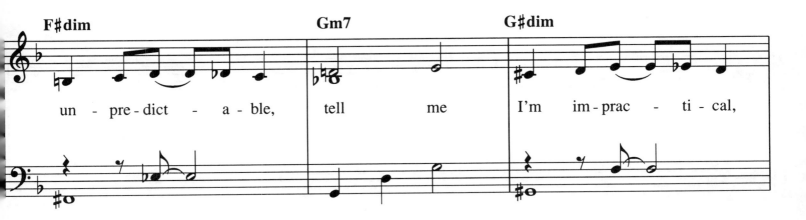

un - pre - dict - a - ble, tell me I'm im - prac - ti - cal,

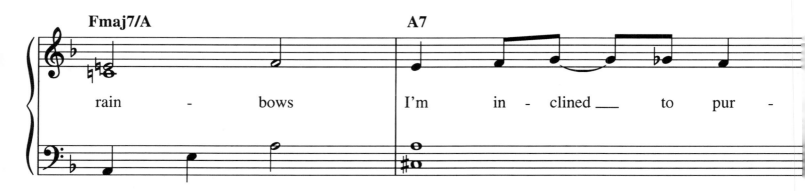

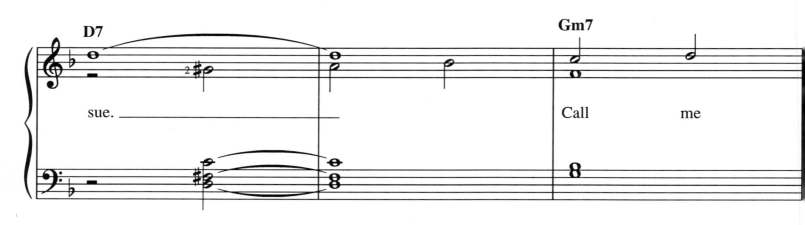

un - de - ni - a - bly true,

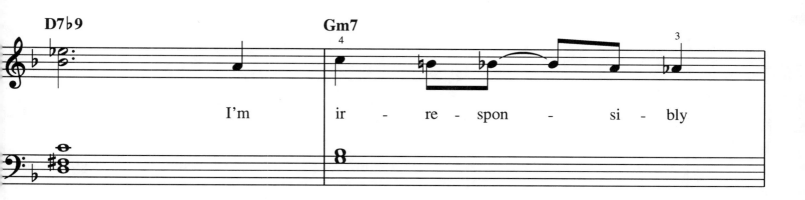

I'm ir - re - spon - si - bly

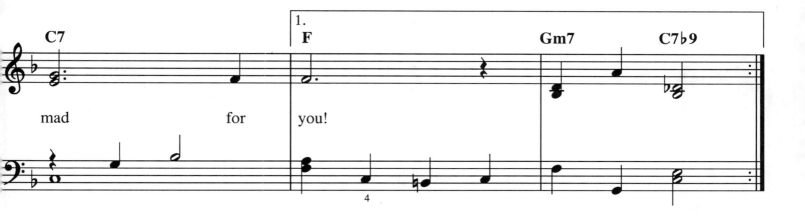

mad for you!

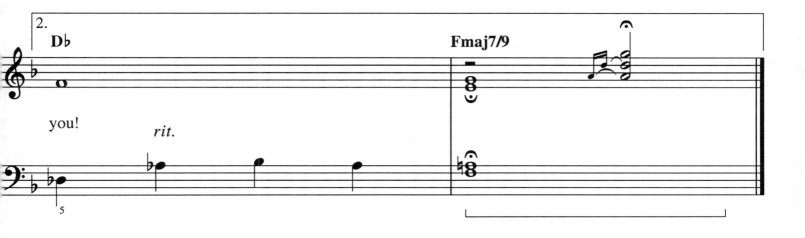

you!   *rit.*

CHERRY PINK AND APPLE BLOSSOM WHITE

from UNDERWATER

French Words by JACQUES LARUE
English Words by MACK DAVID
Music by LOUIGUY

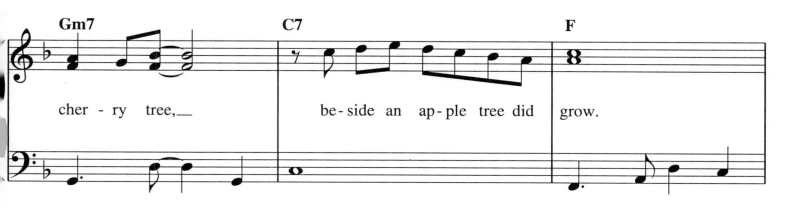

cher - ry tree,___ be - side an ap - ple tree did grow.

And there a boy once met his bride to be___ long long a -

go. The boy looked in - to her eyes, it was a sight to en - thrall, the breez - es

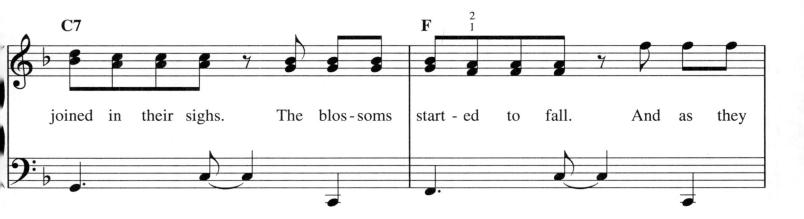

joined in their sighs. The blos - soms start - ed to fall. And as they

gent-ly ca-ressed, the lov-ers | looked up to find, the branch-es | of the two trees were in-ter-

twined. And that is why the po-ets | al-ways write,__ | if there's a new moon bright a-

bove, | it's cher-ry pink and ap-ple | blos-som white,__

when you're in | love.

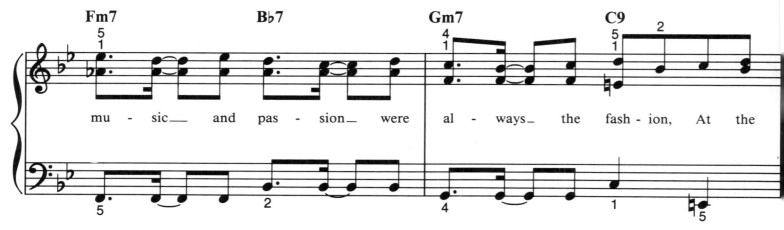

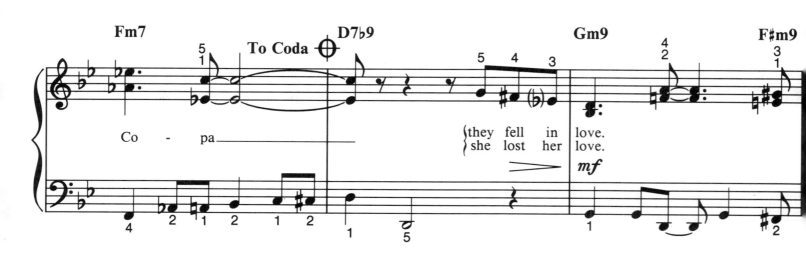

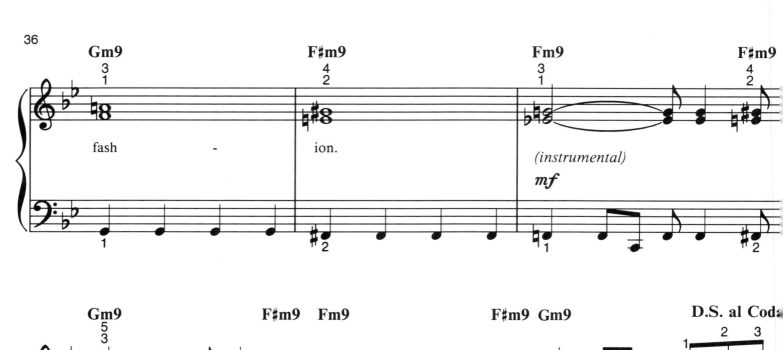

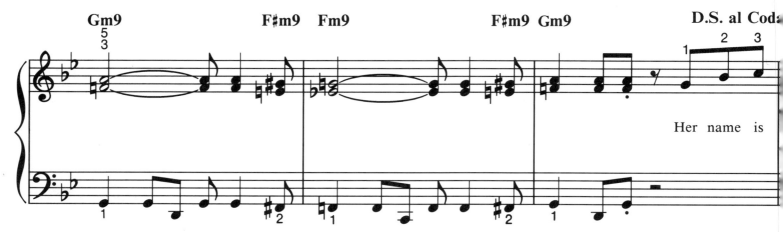

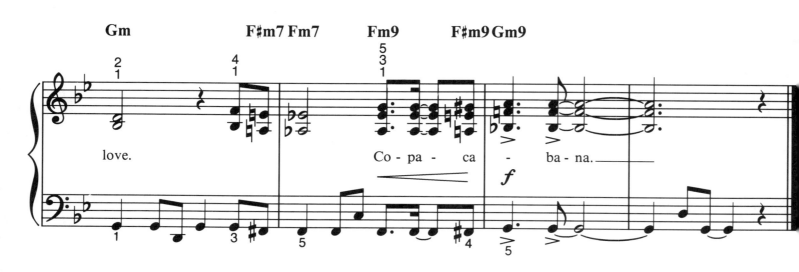

CRY ME A RIVER

Words and Music by
ARTHUR HAMILTON

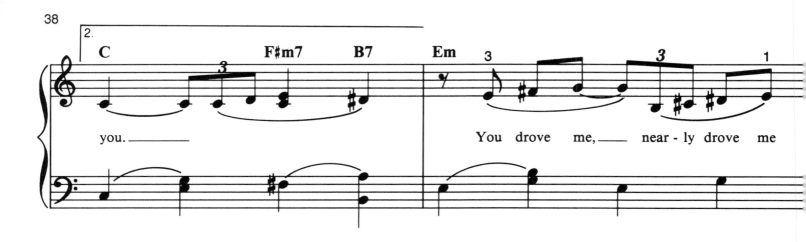

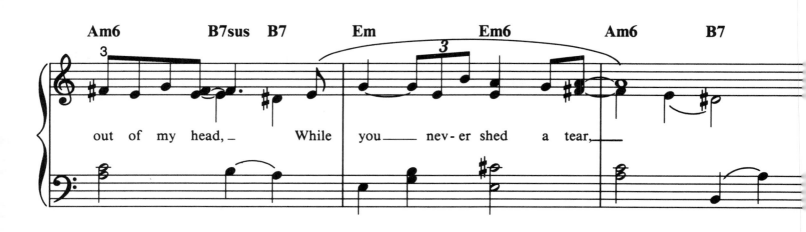

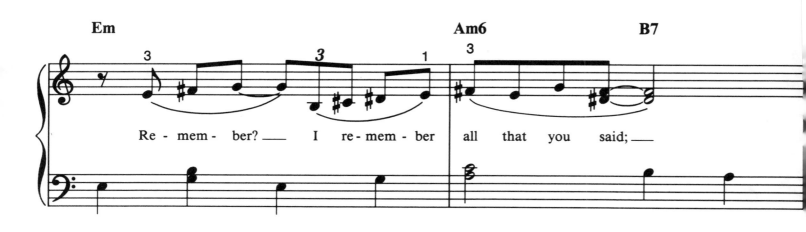

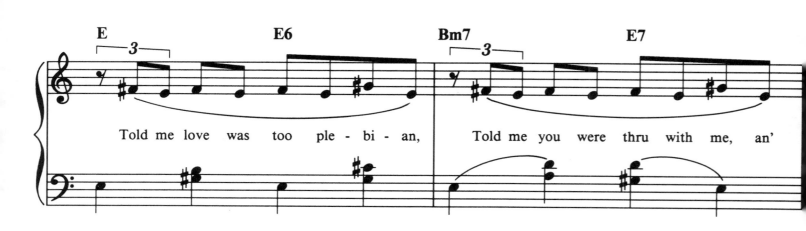

Now _____ you say you love me, _____

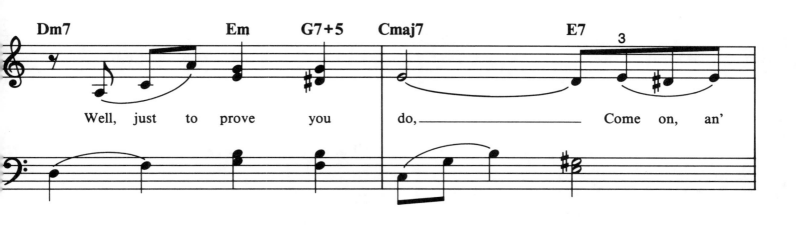

Well, just to prove you do, _____ Come on, an'

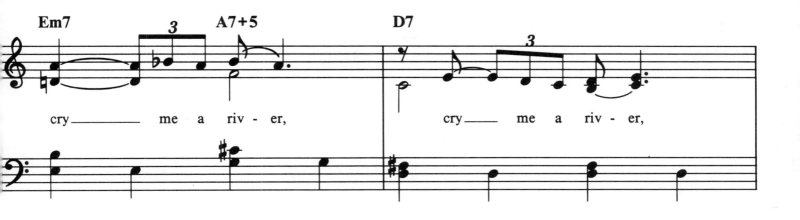

cry _____ me a riv - er, cry _____ me a riv - er,

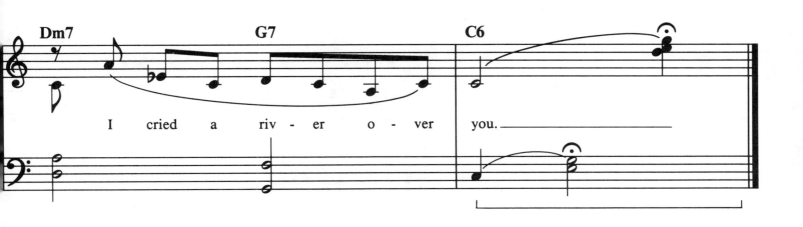

I cried a riv - er o - ver you. _____

DANKE SCHOEN

Lyrics by KURT SCHWABACH and MILT GABLER
Music by BERT KAEMPFERT

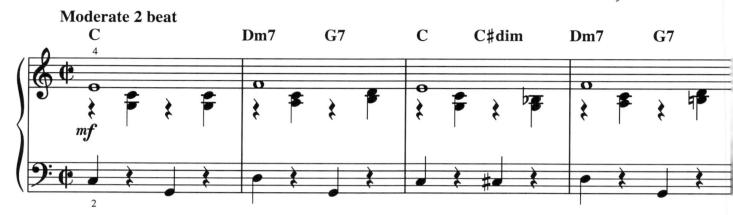

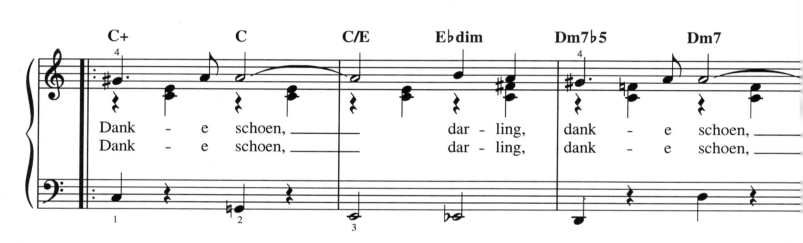

Dank - e schoen, _____ dar - ling, dank - e schoen, _____
Dank - e schoen, _____ dar - ling, dank - e schoen, _____

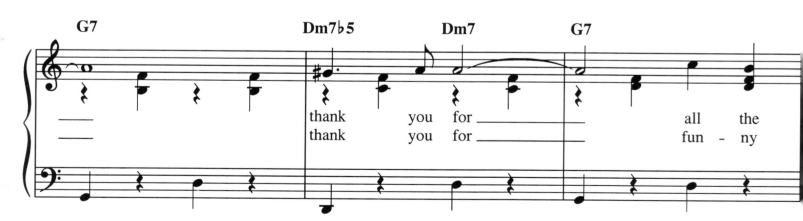

thank you for _____ all the
thank you for _____ fun - ny

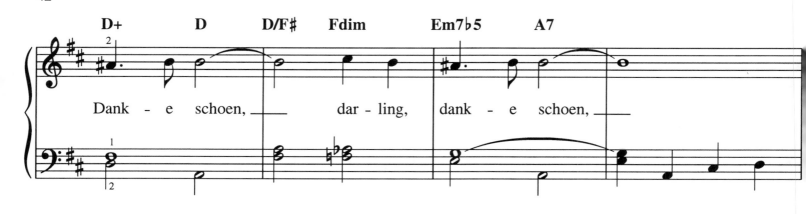

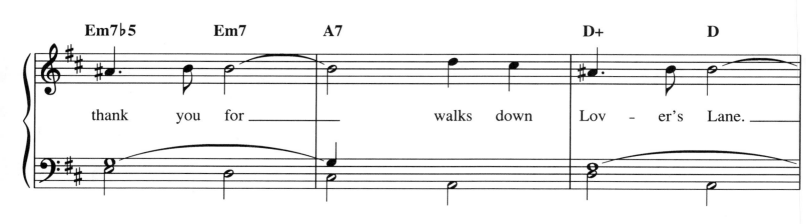

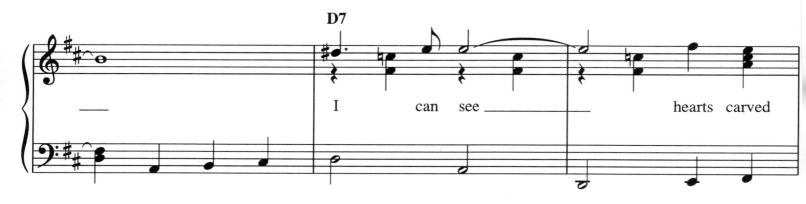

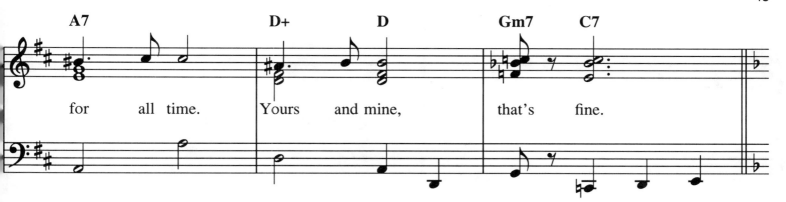

for all time. Yours and mine, that's fine.

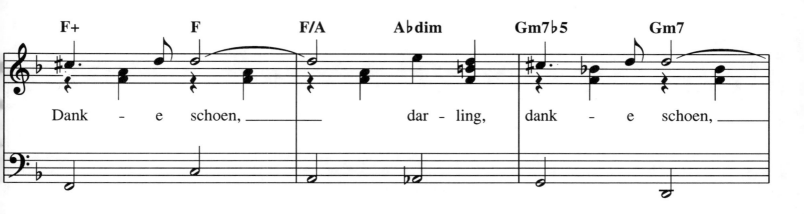

Dank - e schoen, _____ dar - ling, dank - e schoen, _____

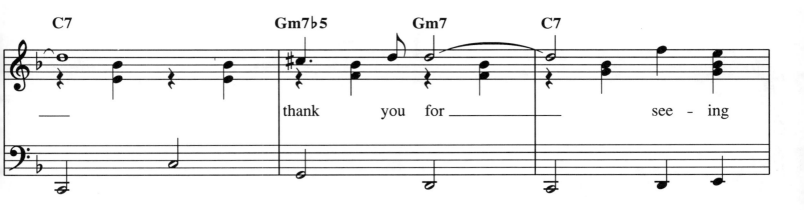

_____ thank you for _____ _____ see - ing

me a - gain. _____ _____ Tho' we go _____

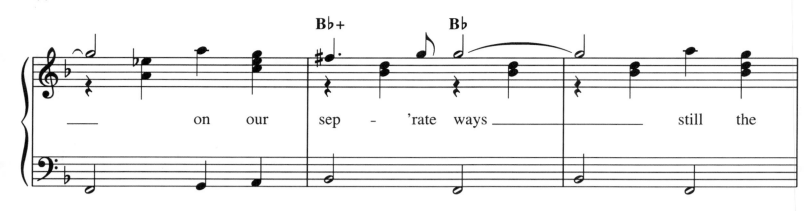

on our sep - 'rate ways ___ still the

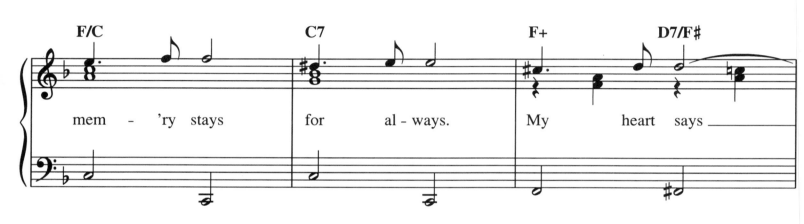

mem - 'ry stays for al - ways. My heart says ___

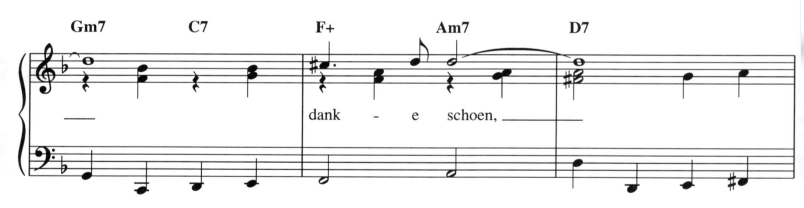

___ dank - e schoen, ___

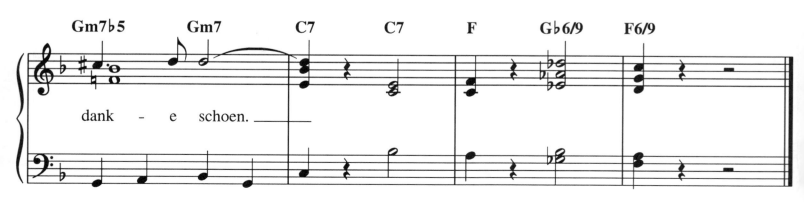

dank - e schoen. ___

DOWNTOWN

Words and Music by
TONY HATCH

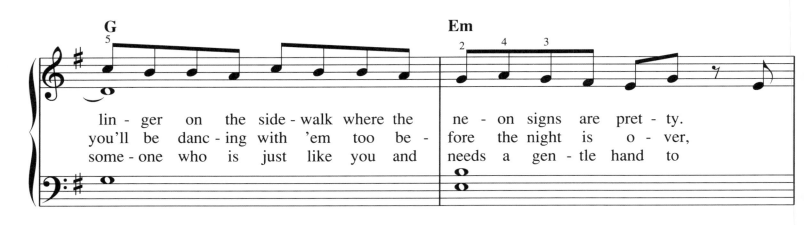

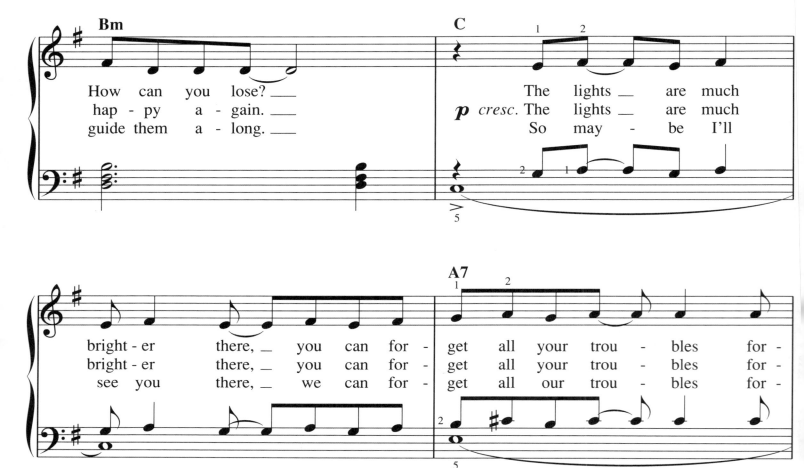

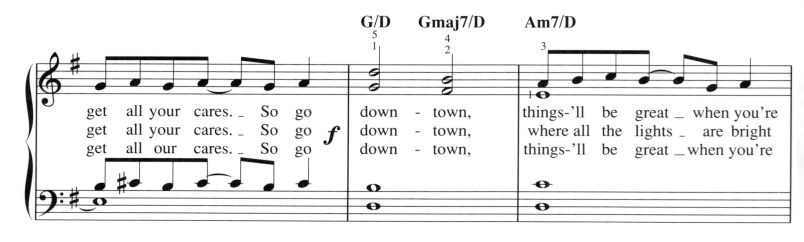

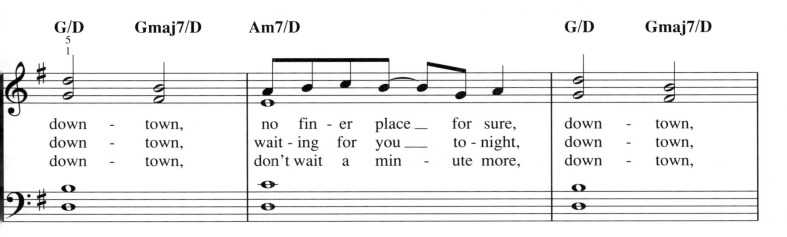

down - town,
down - town,
down - town,

no fin - er place __ for sure,
wait - ing for you __ to - night,
don't wait a min - ute more,

down - town,
down - town,
down - town,

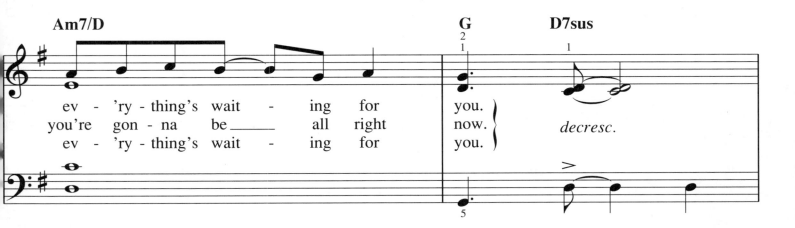

ev - 'ry - thing's wait - ing for
you're gon - na be ____ all right
ev - 'ry - thing's wait - ing for

you.
now.
you.

decresc.

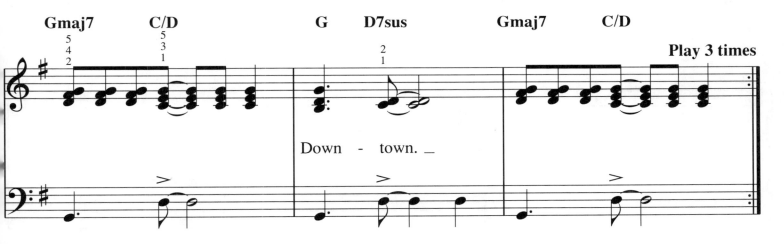

Play 3 times

Down - town. __

Repeat and Fade

Down - town, __

Down - town. __

ppp

DON'T CRY FOR ME ARGENTINA

from EVITA

Words by TIM RICE
Music by ANDREW LLOYD WEBBER

Moderate Tango tempo

It won't be eas-y, you'll think it strange When I try to ex-plain how I feel, That I still need your love af-ter all that I've done. You won't be-lieve me; All you will see is a girl you once knew al-though she's dressed up to the

MCA Music Publishing

nines at six - es and sev - ens with you.

I had to let it hap - pen, I had to change; Could - n't

And as for for - tune and as for fame,

I

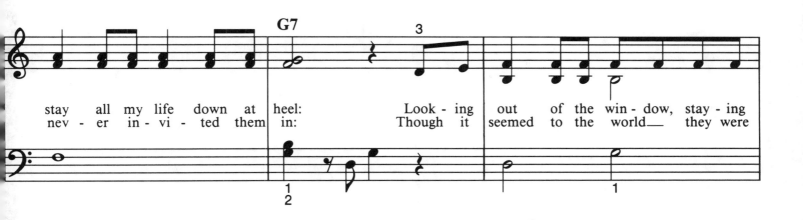

stay all my life down at heel: Look - ing out of the win - dow, stay - ing

nev - er in - vi - ted them in: Though it seemed to the world___ they were

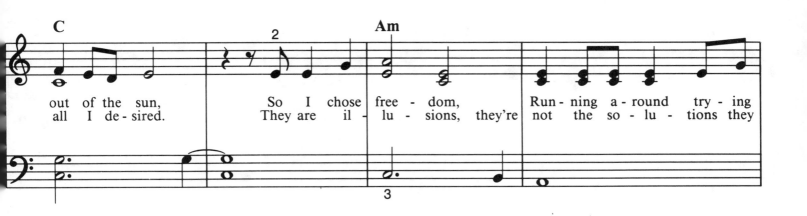

out of the sun, So I chose free - dom, Run - ning a - round try - ing

all I de - sired. They are il - lu - sions, they're not the so - lu - tions they

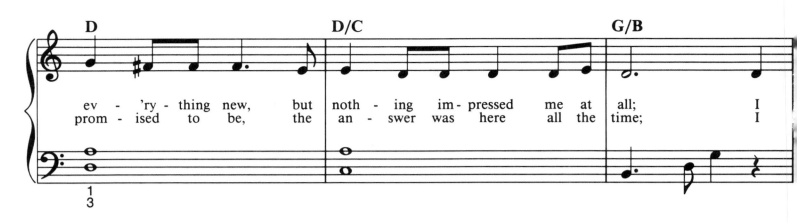

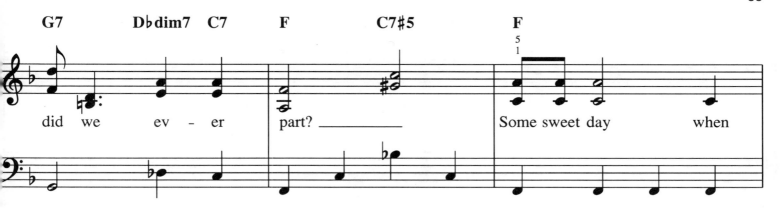

did we ev – er part? _____ Some sweet day when

blos-soms fall and all the world's a song, _____

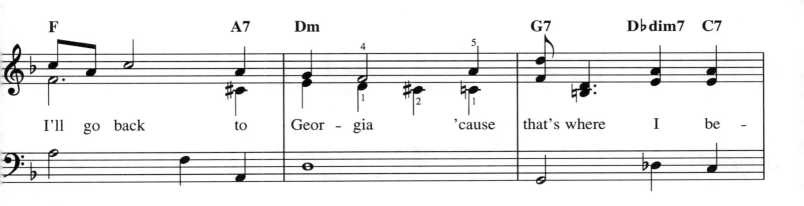

I'll go back to Geor - gia 'cause that's where I be -

long. Geor - gia, ___ Geor - gia, ___

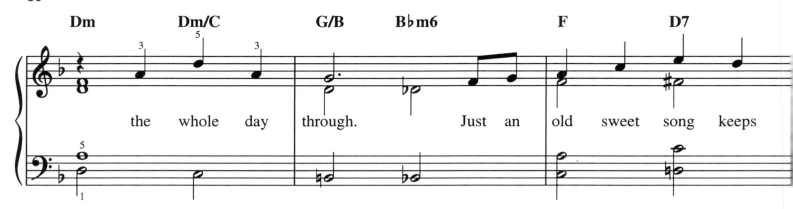

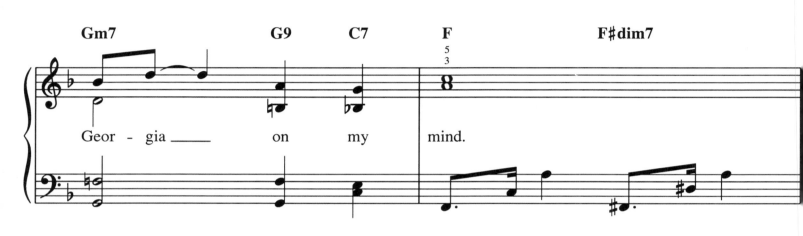

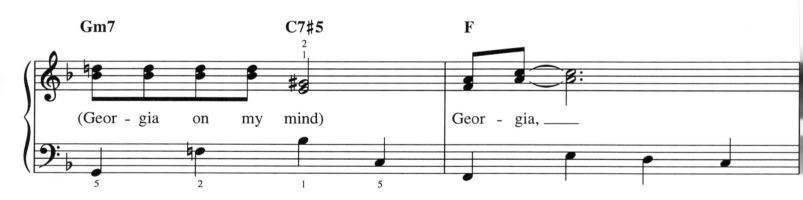

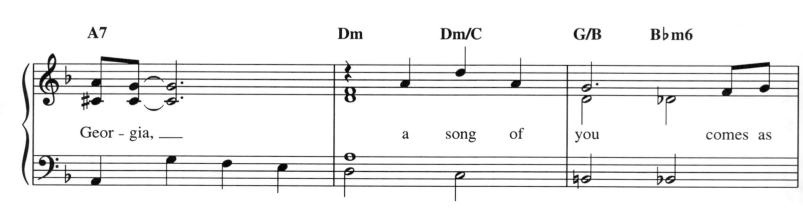

sweet and clear as moon-light through the pines. _____

_____ Oth - er arms ___ reach out to me, ___

oth - er eyes ___ smile ten - der - ly, ___

still in peace - ful dreams I see _____ the

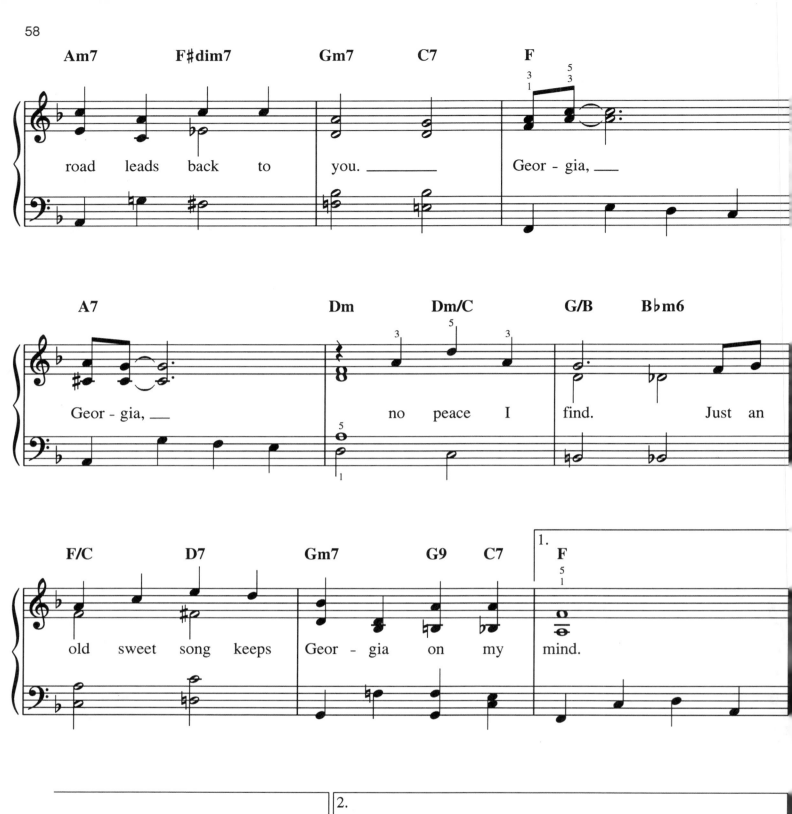

THE GIRL FROM IPANEMA
(Garôta De Ipanema)

English Words by NORMAN GIMBEL
Original Words by VINICIUS DE MORAES
Music by ANTONIO CARLOS JOBIM

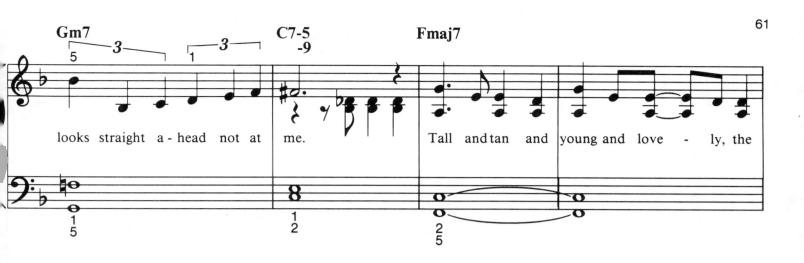

looks straight a - head not at me. Tall and tan and young and love - ly, the

girl from I - pa - ne - ma goes walk - ing, and when she pass - es I

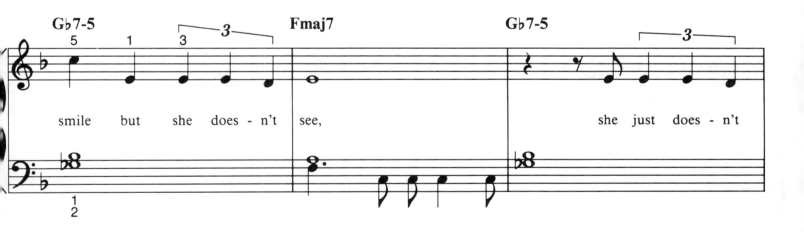

smile but she does - n't see, she just does - n't

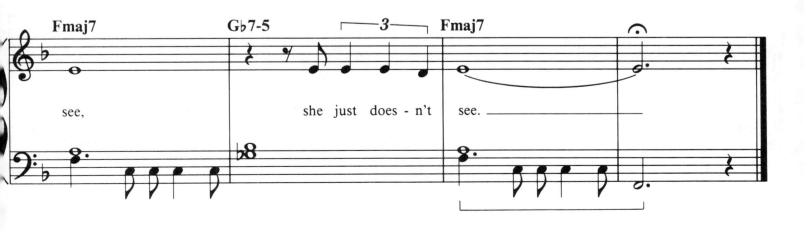

see, she just does - n't see. _____

THE GLORY OF LOVE

Words and Music by
BILLY HILL

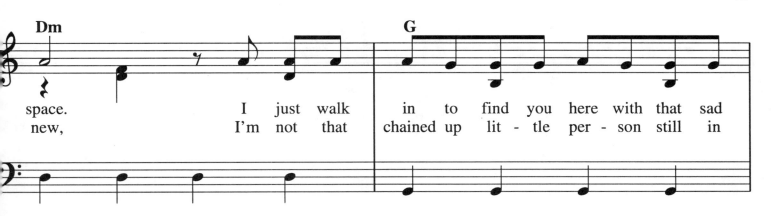

space.   I   just   walk   in   to   find   you   here   with   that   sad
new,   I'm   not   that   chained   up   lit - tle   per - son   still   in

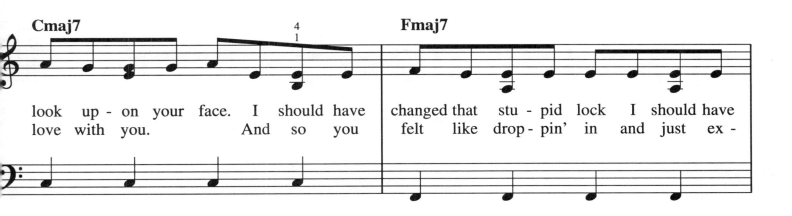

look   up - on   your   face.   I   should   have   changed   that   stu - pid   lock   I   should   have
love   with   you.   And   so   you   felt   like   drop - pin'   in   and   just   ex -

made   you   leave   your   key   if   I'd - 've   known   for   just   one   sec - ond   you'd   be
pect   me   to   be   free. Well   now,   I'm   sav - in'   all   my   lov - in'   for   some -

back   to   both - er   me. Go   on,   now   go,   walk   out   the   door   just   turn   a -
one   who's   lov - in'   me. Go   on,   now

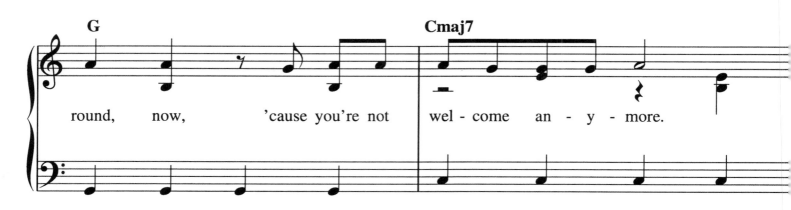

G **Cmaj7**

round, now, 'cause you're not wel - come an - y - more.

Fmaj7 4 **Bm7♭5**

weren't you the one who tried to hurt me with good-bye? Did you think I'd

E7sus 2 **E7** 3 4

crum - ble, did you think I'd lay down and die. Oh no, not

Am 5 3 **Dm** 5 3

I, I will sur - vive.___ Oh, as

I WRITE THE SONGS

Words and Music by
BRUCE JOHNSTON

IT'S NOT UNUSUAL

Words and Music by GORDON MILLS
and LES REED

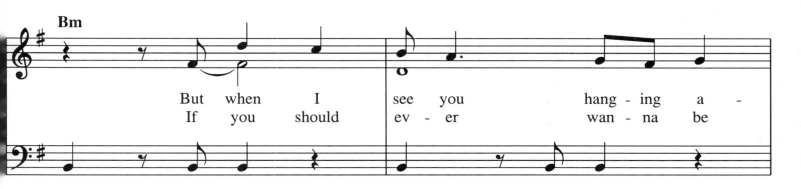

Bm

But when I see you hang - ing a -
If you should ev - er wan - na be

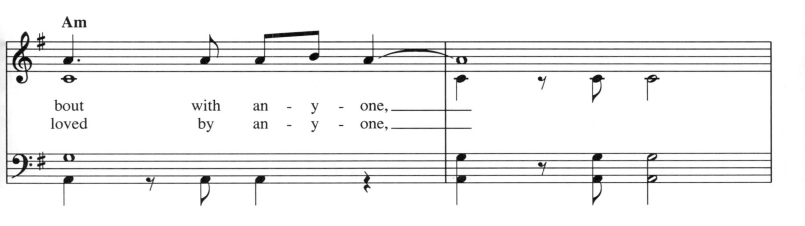

Am

bout with an - y - one,_____
loved by an - y - one,_____

D7   **1.** **G**

It's not un - u - su - al _____ to see me cry. _____
It's not un - u - su - al _____ it

Am7   **D7**

I wan - na die. _____

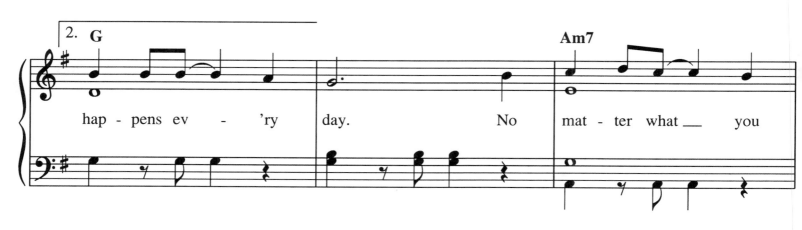

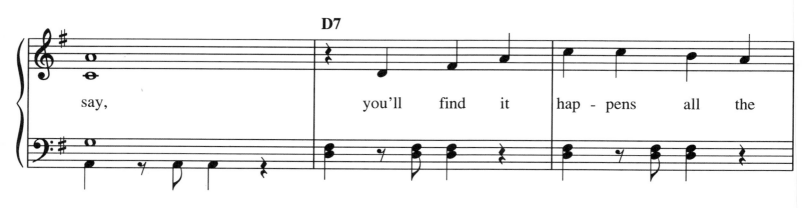

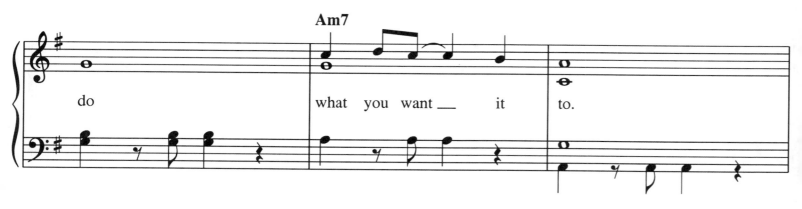

D7

Why can't this cra - zy love be mine?_____

Bb7   **Am7**   **D7**

G   **Am7**

It's not un - u - su - al___ to be mad with an - y - one.___

D7   **G**

___ It's not un - u - su - al___ to be

IF

Words and Music by
DAVID GATES

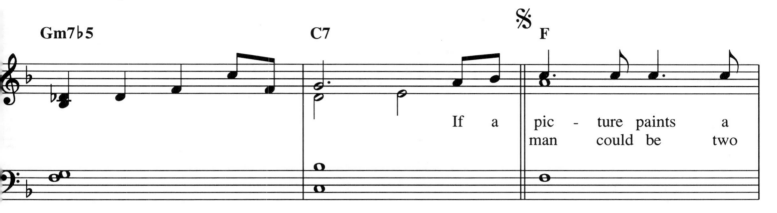

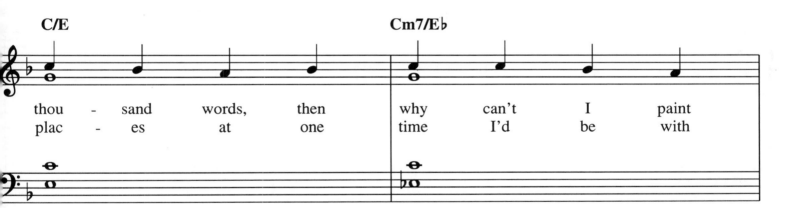

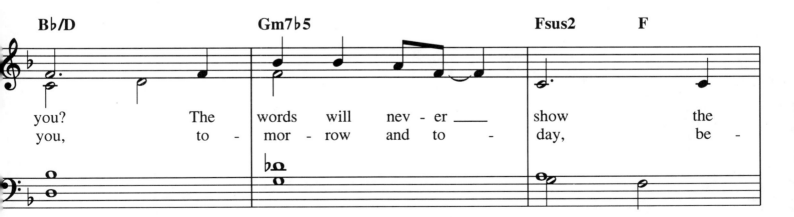

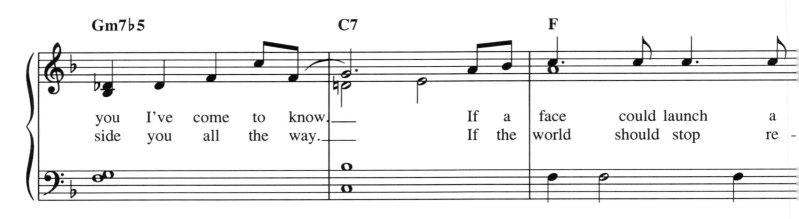

Gm7♭5   **C7**   **F**

you I've come to know. If a face could launch a
side you all the way. If the world should stop re -

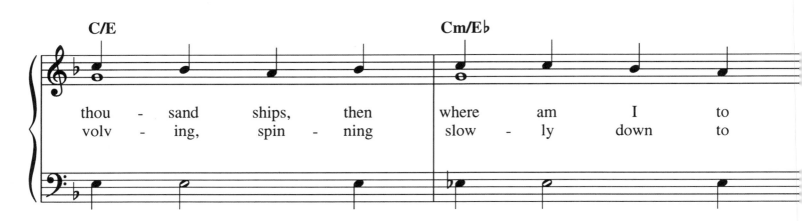

C/E   **Cm/E♭**

thou - sand ships, then where am I to
volv - ing, spin - ning slow - ly down to

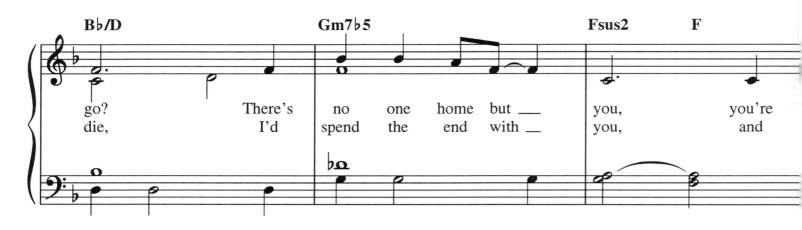

B♭/D   **Gm7♭5**   **Fsus2**   **F**

go? There's no one home but ___ you, you're
die, I'd spend the end with ___ you, and

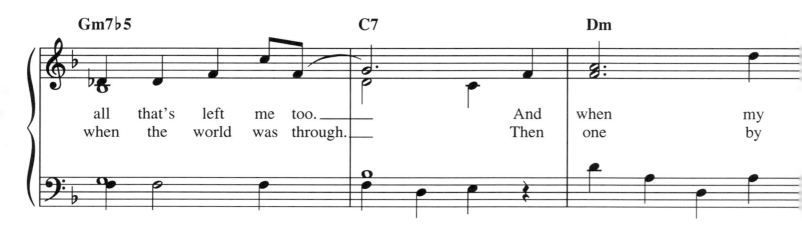

Gm7♭5   **C7**   **Dm**

all that's left me too. And when my
when the world was through. Then one by

THE LADY IS A TRAMP

from BABES IN ARMS

Words by LORENZ HART
Music by RICHARD RODGERS

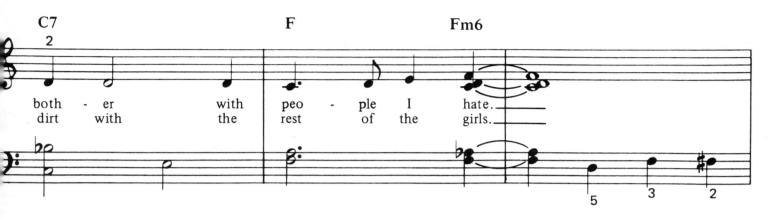

both - er   with   peo - ple I hate.
dirt with   the   rest of the girls.

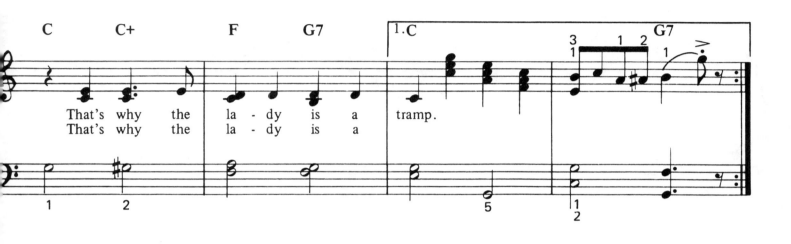

That's why the la - dy is a tramp.
That's why the la - dy is a

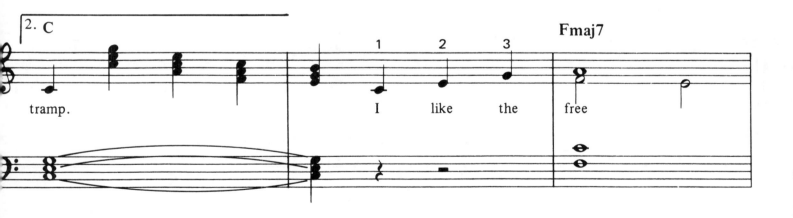

tramp.   I like the free

fresh   wind in my hair,

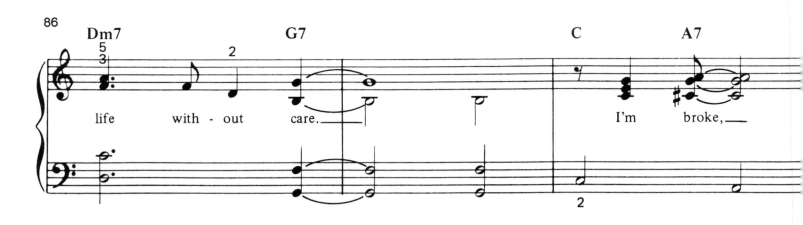

life with - out care. I'm broke,___

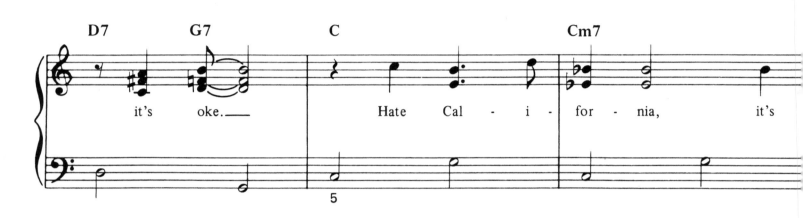

it's oke.___ Hate Cal - i - for - nia, it's

cold and it's damp.___ That's why the

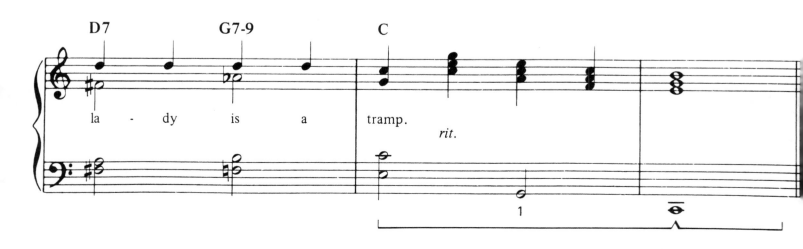

la - dy is a tramp.

rit.

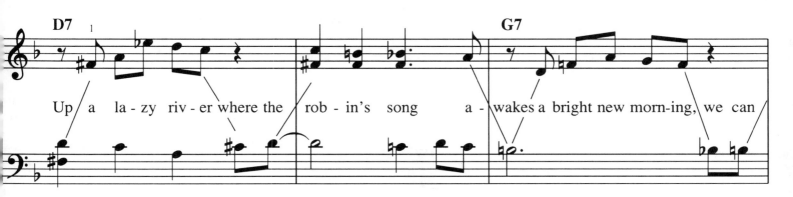

Up a la - zy riv - er where the rob - in's song a - wakes a bright new morn - ing, we can

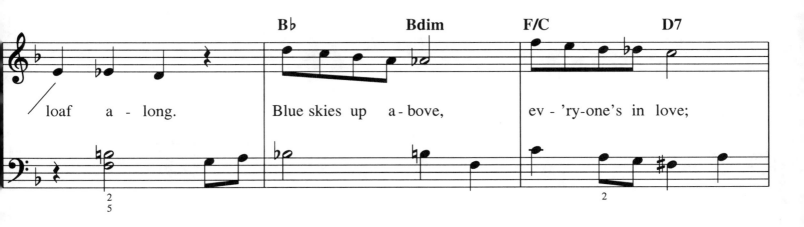

loaf a - long. Blue skies up a - bove, ev - 'ry-one's in love;

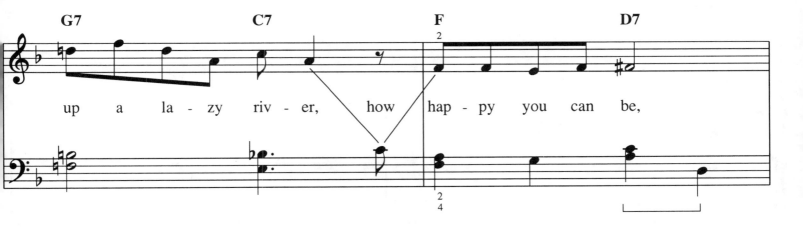

up a la - zy riv - er, how hap - py you can be,

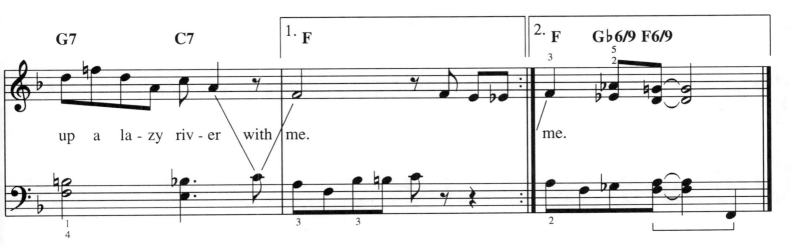

up a la - zy riv - er with me. me.

L-O-V-E

Words and Music by BERT KAEMPFERT
and MILT GABLER

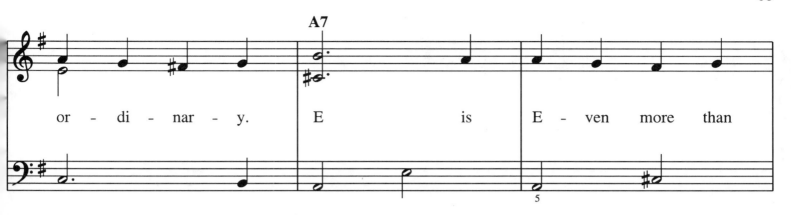

or - di - nar - y. E is E - ven more than

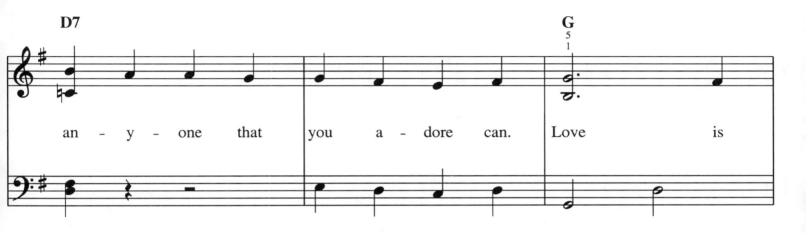

an - y - one that you a - dore can. Love is

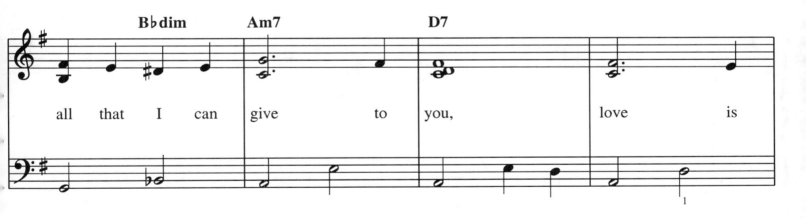

all that I can give to you, love is

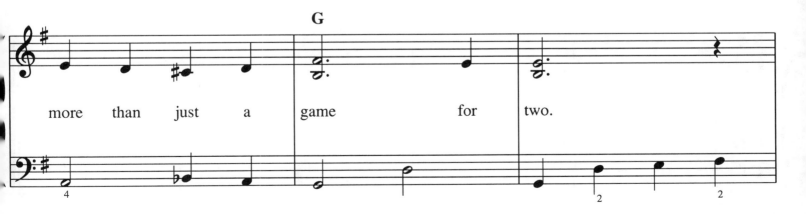

more than just a game for two.

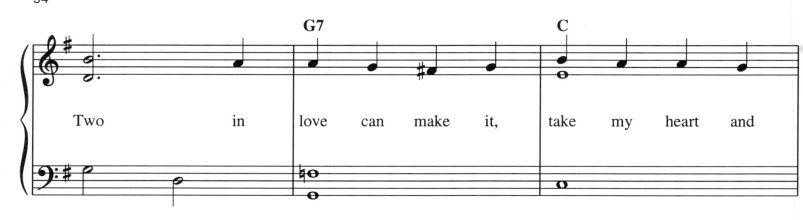

Two in love can make it, take my heart and

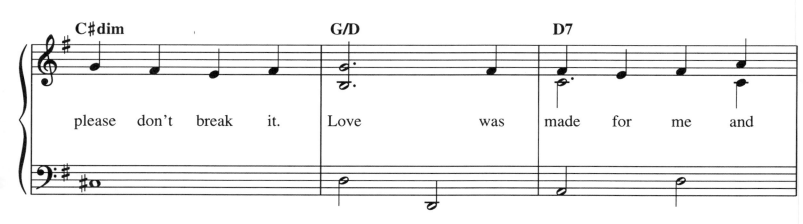

please don't break it. Love was made for me and

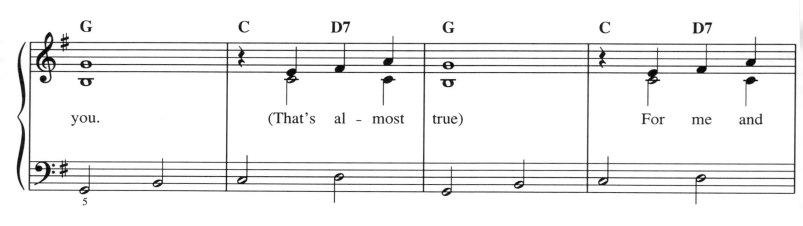

you. (That's al - most true) For me and

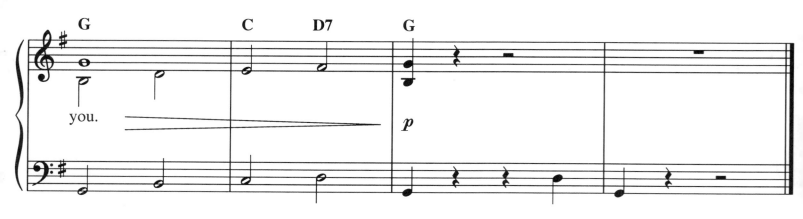

you.

MANDY

Words and Music by SCOTT ENGLISH
and RICHARD KERR

Moderately

I re-mem-ber all my life
morn-ing, just an-oth-er day.

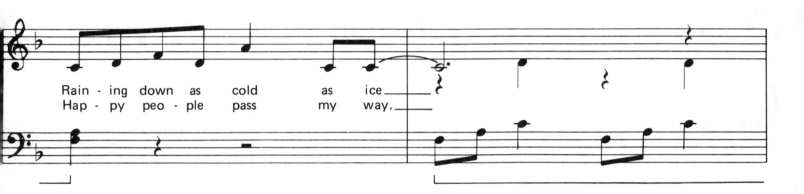

Rain-ing down as cold as ice
Hap-py peo-ple pass my way.

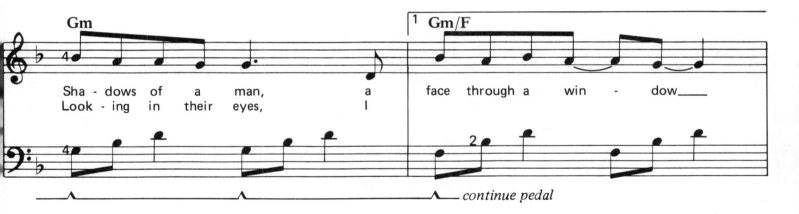

Sha-dows of a man, a
Look-ing in their eyes, I

face through a win-dow

continue pedal

cry-in' in the night. The night turns in-to
see a mem-'ry, I

nev-er re-al-ized how hap-py you made_ me. Oh, Man - dy, Well, you came_

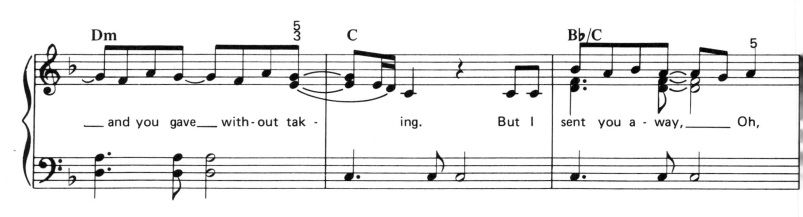

_ and you gave_ with-out tak - ing. But I sent you a - way,_ Oh,

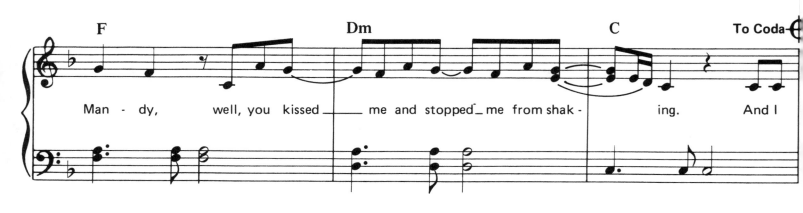

Man - dy, well, you kissed_ me and stopped_ me from shak - ing. And I

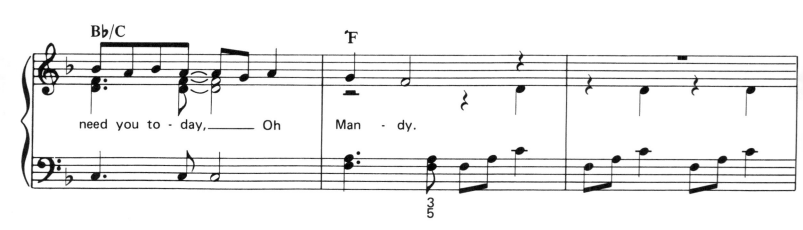

need you to - day,_ Oh Man - dy.

Stand-ing on the edge of time____ walked a-way when love was mine.___

Gm   **Gm/F**

Caught up in a world of up-hill climb-ing;

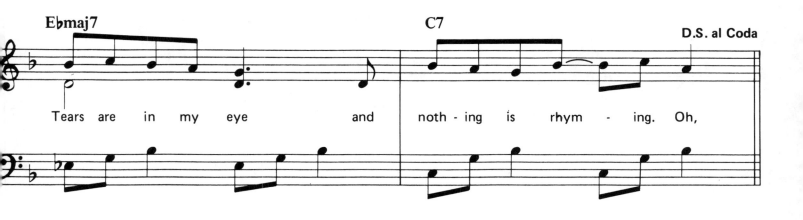

E♭maj7   **C7**   **D.S. al Coda**

Tears are in my eye and noth-ing is rhym - ing. Oh,

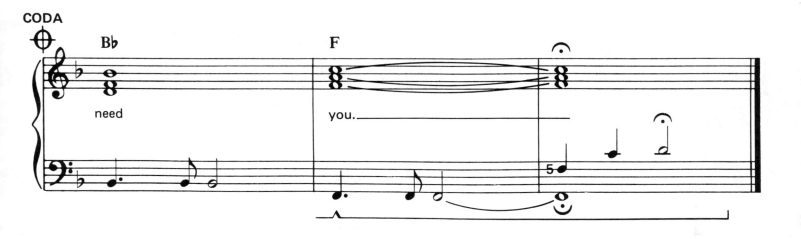

CODA

B♭   **F**

need you.____

LOVE WILL KEEP US TOGETHER

Words and Music by NEIL SEDAKA
and HOWARD GREENFIELD

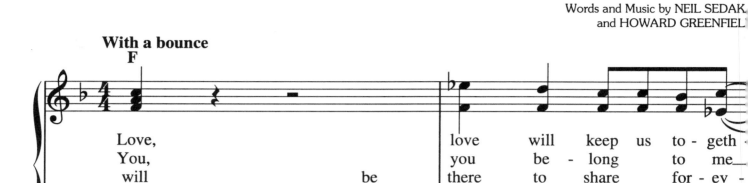

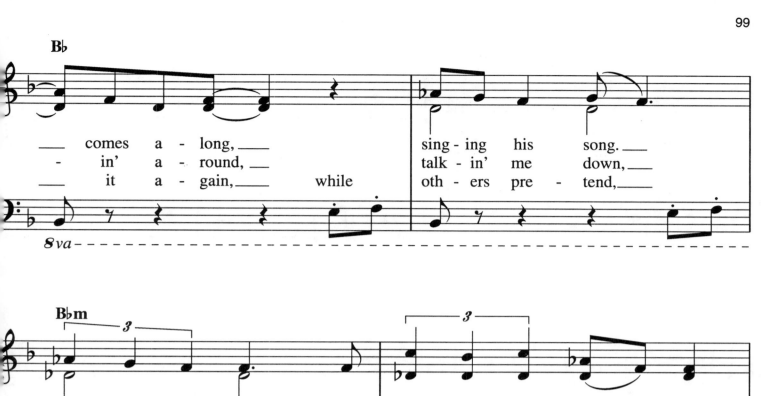

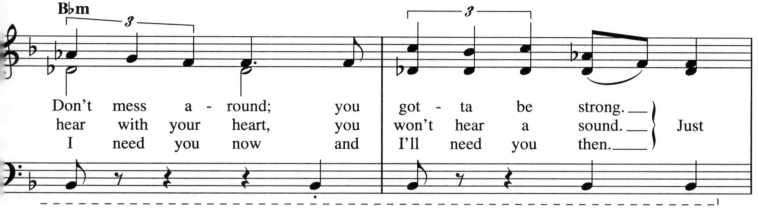

MICHELLE

Words and Music by JOHN LENNO
and PAUL McCARTNE

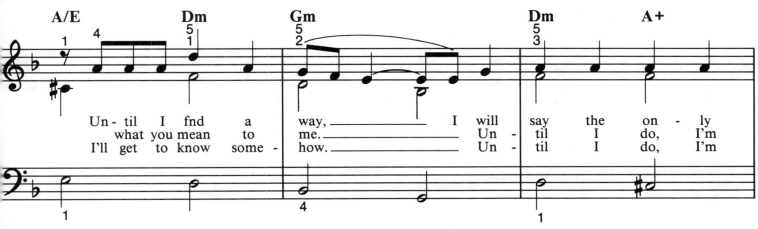

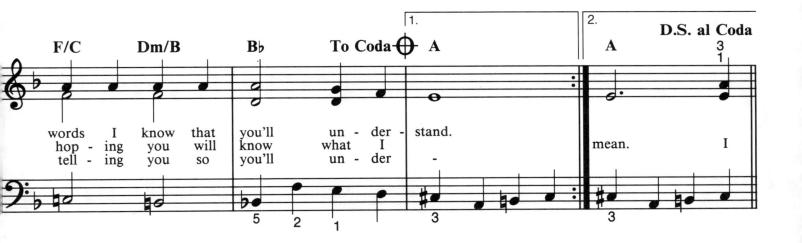

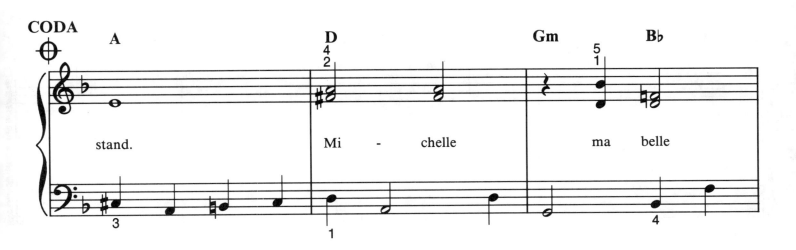

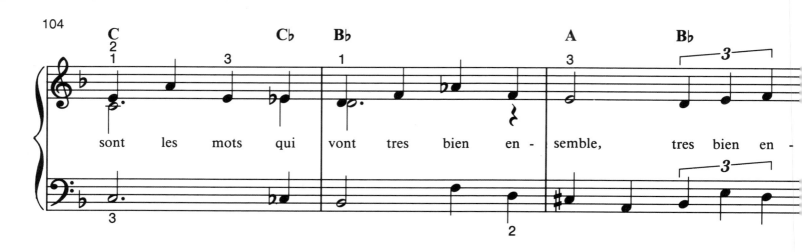

sont les mots qui vont tres bien en - semble, tres bien en -

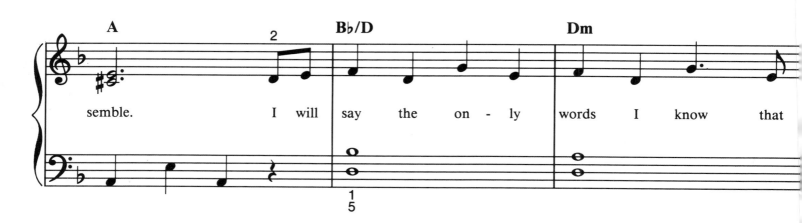

semble. I will say the on - ly words I know that

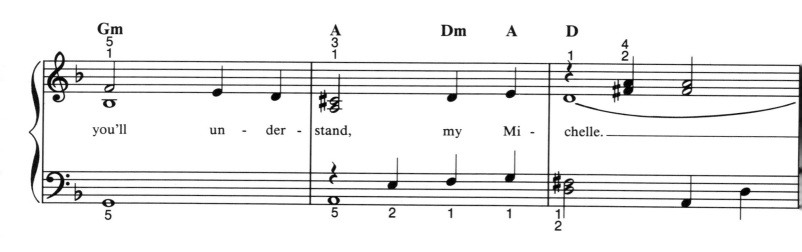

you'll un - der - stand, my Mi - chelle.

rit. e dim.

MONA LISA

from the Paramount Picture CAPTAIN CAREY, U.S.A.

Words and Music by JAY LIVINGSTON
and RAY EVANS

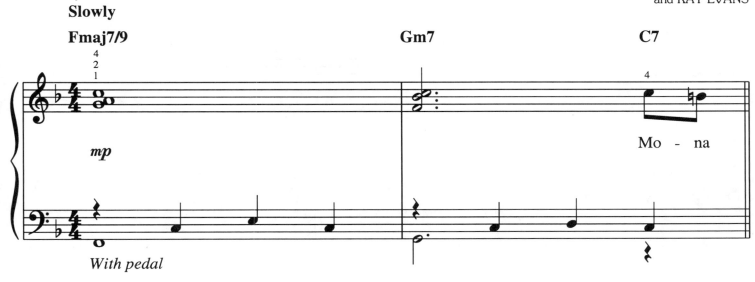

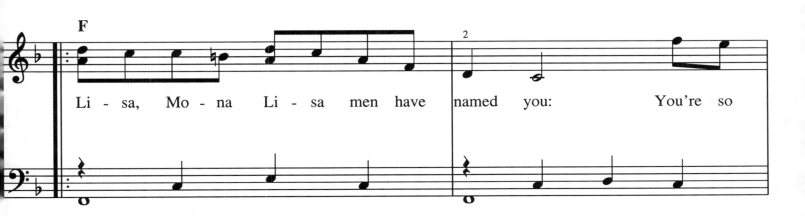

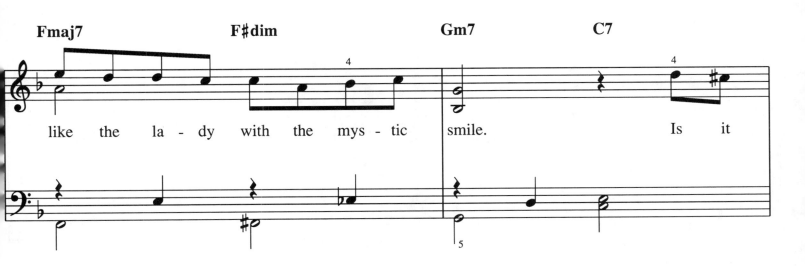

MISTY

Words by JOHNNY BURKE
Music by ERROLL GARNER

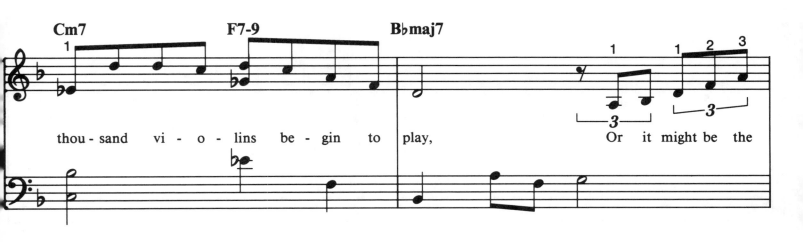

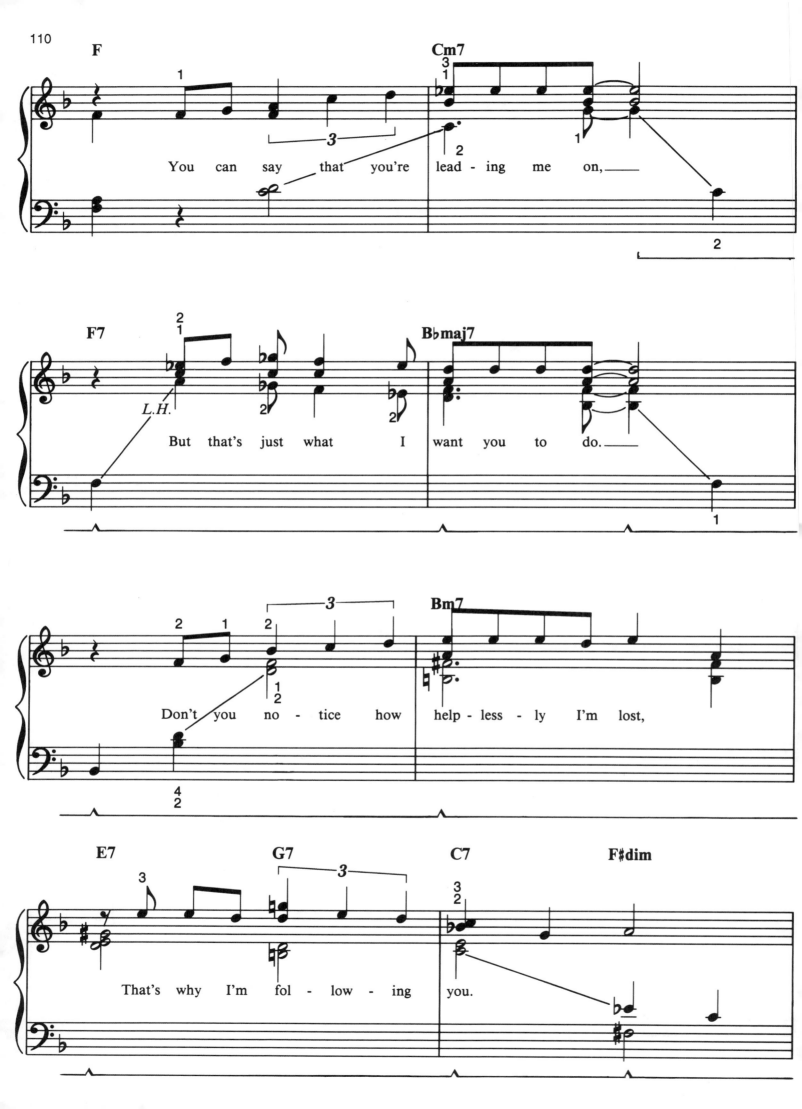

MOON RIVER

from the Paramount Picture BREAKFAST AT TIFFANY'S

Words by JOHNNY MERCER
Music by HENRY MANCINI

ON A CLEAR DAY
(You Can See Forever)

Lyrics by ALAN JAY LERNER
Music by BURTON LANE

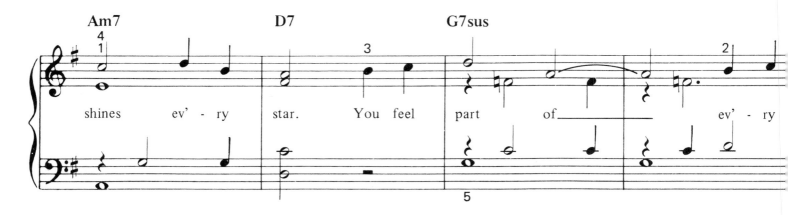

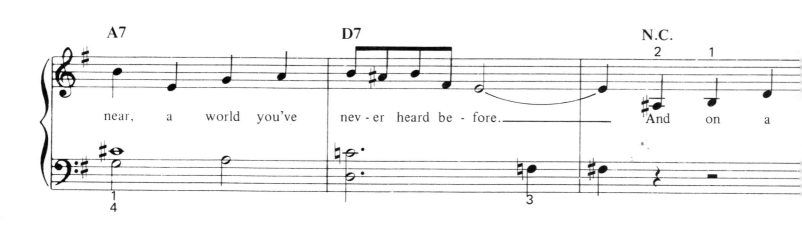

ROUTE 66

By BOBBY TROUP

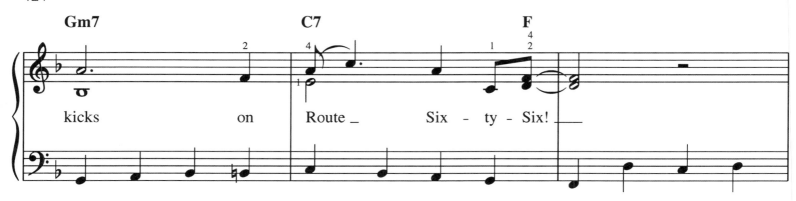

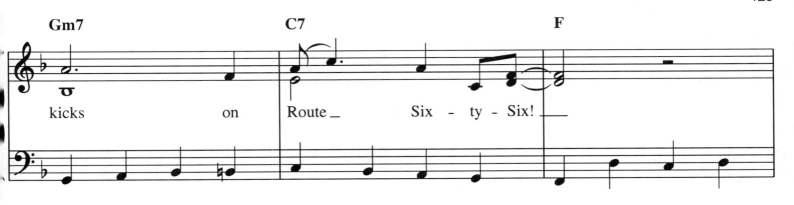

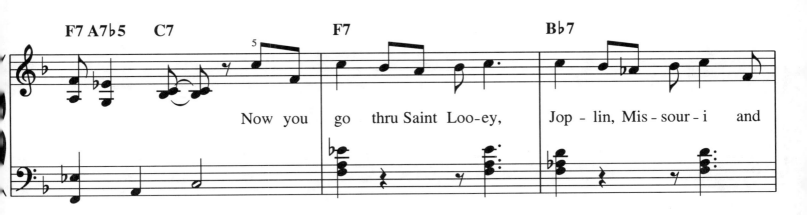

Mex - i - co; _____ Flag - staff, Ar - i - zon - a;

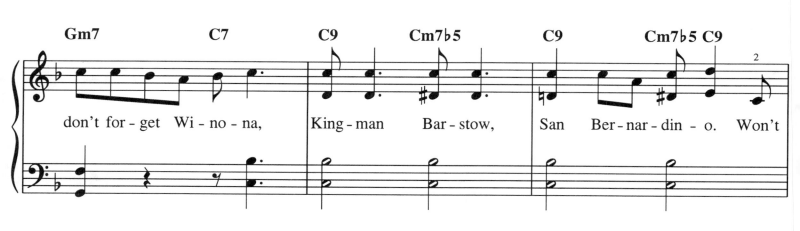

don't for - get Wi - no - na, King - man Bar - stow, San Ber - nar - din - o. Won't

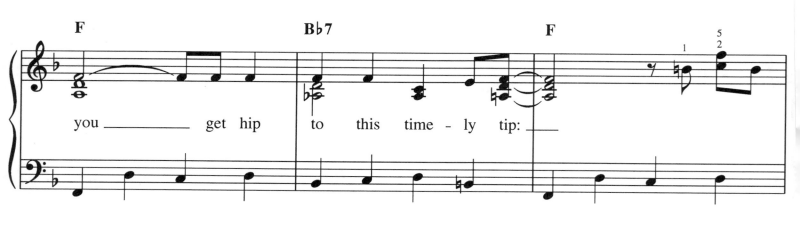

you _____ get hip to this time - ly tip: _____

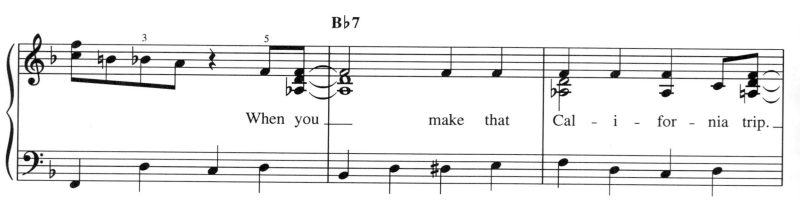

When you _____ make that Cal - i - for - nia trip.

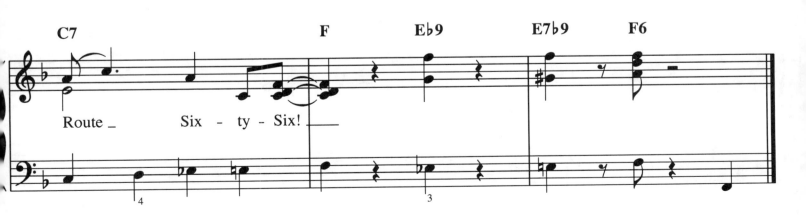

SCOTCH AND SODA

Words and Music by
DAVE GUARD

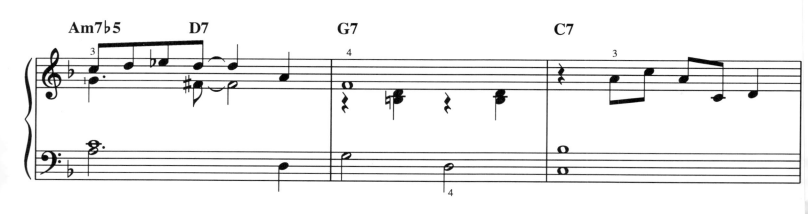

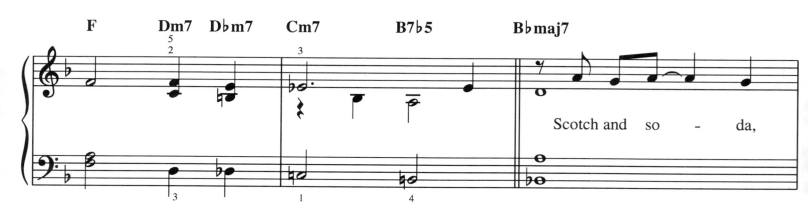

Scotch and so - da,

mud in your eye, __   ba-by, do I feel   high,   oh   me, __   oh

my,   do __ I __ feel   high.

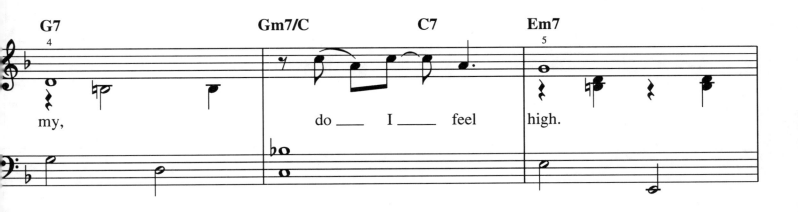

Dry mar - tin - i,   jig-ger of gin,

oh, what a spell you've   got me   in, __   oh   my,

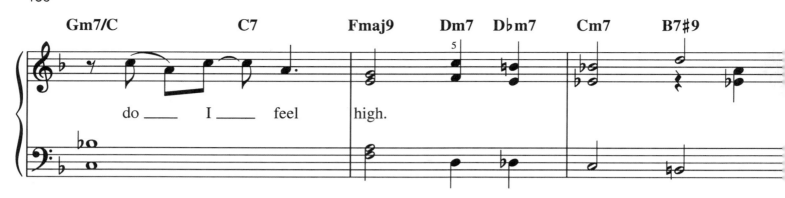

do ___ I ___ feel high.

Peo-ple won't _ be - lieve me. __ They'll think that I'm just

drink-ing. _____ But I could feel __ the way I feel, __ and

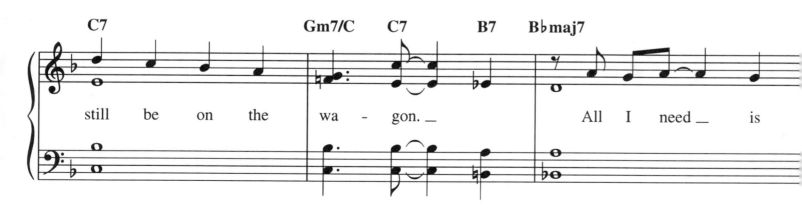

still be on the wa - gon. __ All I need _ is

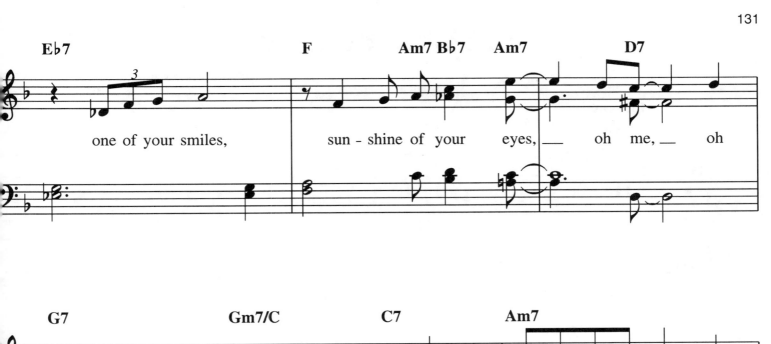

one of your smiles, sun-shine of your eyes, ___ oh me, ___ oh

my, do ___ I ___ feel high-er than a kite can

fly! _____ Give me lov-in', ba-by, I feel

high.

SPANISH EYES

Words by CHARLES SINGLETON and EDDIE SNYDE
Music by BERT KAEMPFER

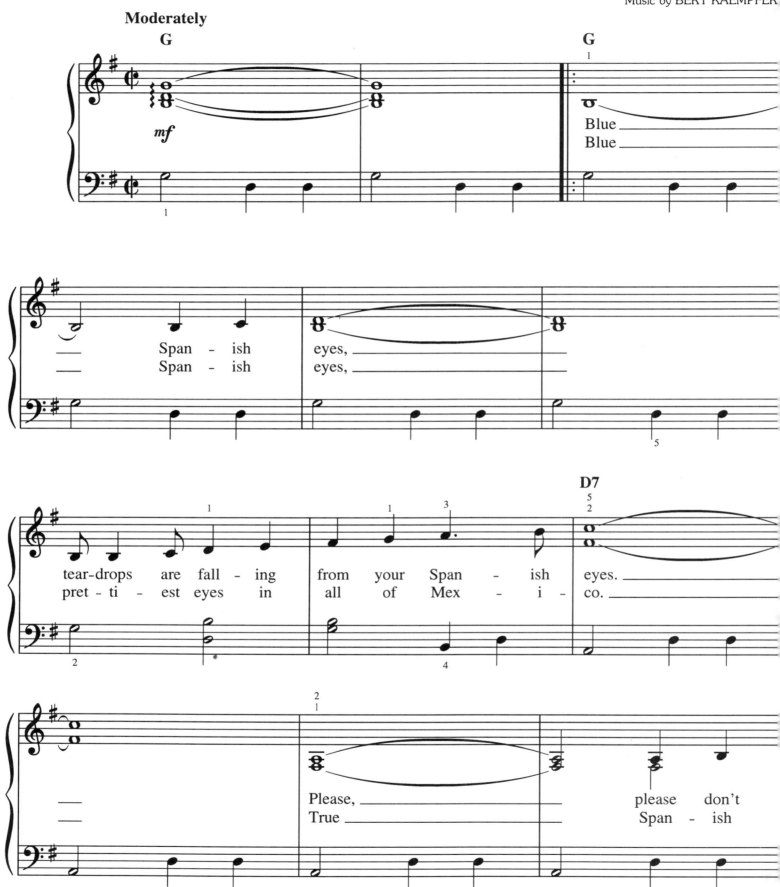

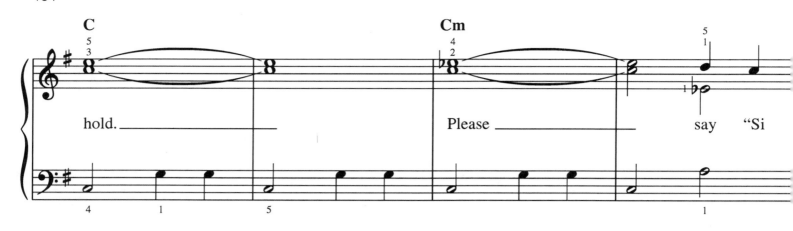

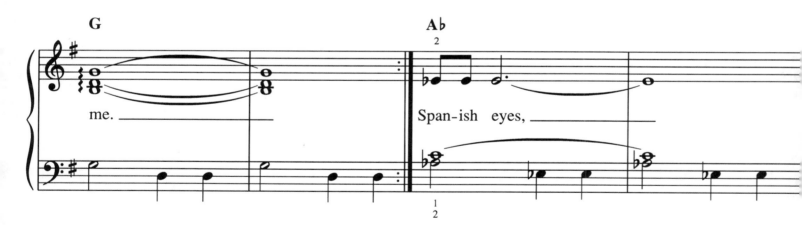

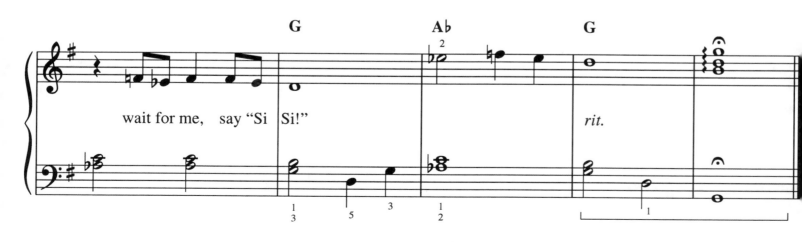

STRANGERS IN THE NIGHT
Adapted from A MAN COULD GET KILLED

Words by CHARLES SINGLETON and EDDIE SNYDER
Music by BERT KAEMPFERT

MCA Music Publishing

C9

some - thing in your smile____ was so ex - cit - ing, some - thing in my heart____

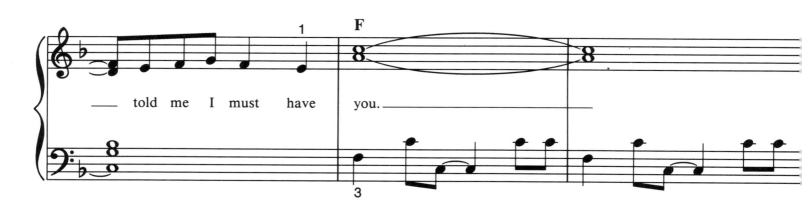

F

____ told me I must have you.____

Cm6 **D7-9**

Stran - gers in the night,____ ____ two lone - ly peo - ple, we were stran - gers in the night

Gm **B♭m**

____ up to the mo - ment when we said our first hel - lo. Lit - tle did we know

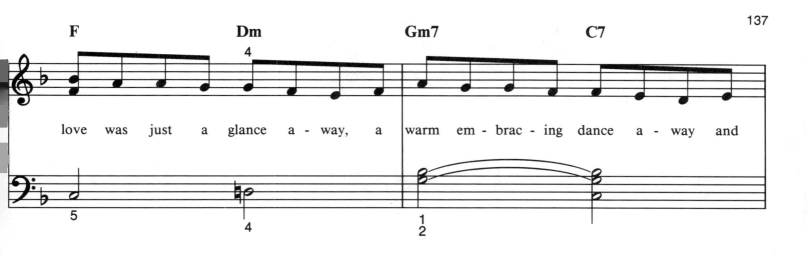

love was just a glance a - way, a warm em - brac - ing dance a - way and

ev - er since that night _____ we've been to - geth - er, lov - ers at first sight, _____

_____ in love for - ev - er; It turned out so right _____ for stran - gers in the

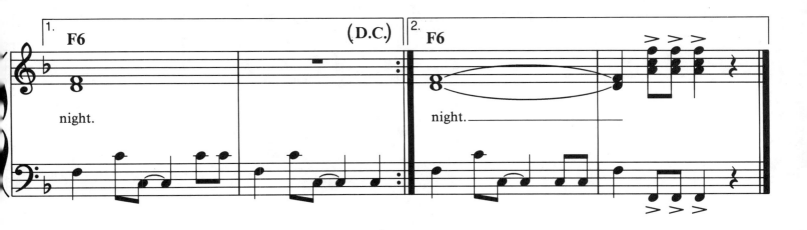

night.   night. _____

SPINNING WHEEL

Words and Music by
DAVID CLAYTON THOMAS

flect - ing   sign?___   Just   let   it   shine___   with -

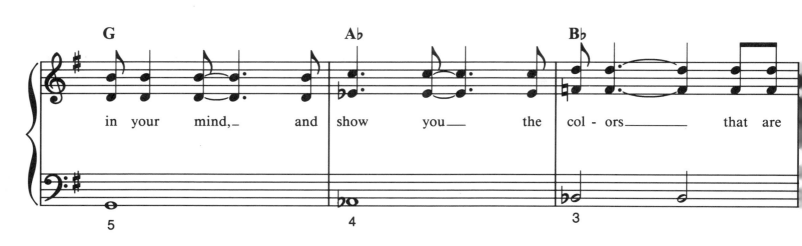

in   your   mind,___   and   show   you___   the   col - ors___   that   are

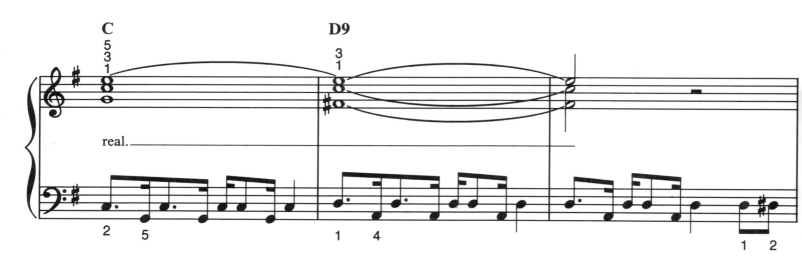

real.___

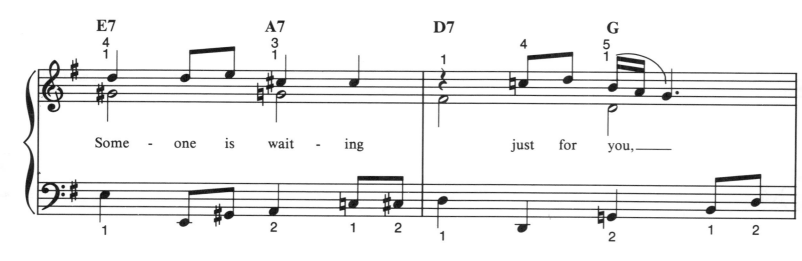

Some - one   is   wait - ing   just   for   you,___

THAT'S LIFE

Words and Music by DEAN KAY
and KELLY GORDON

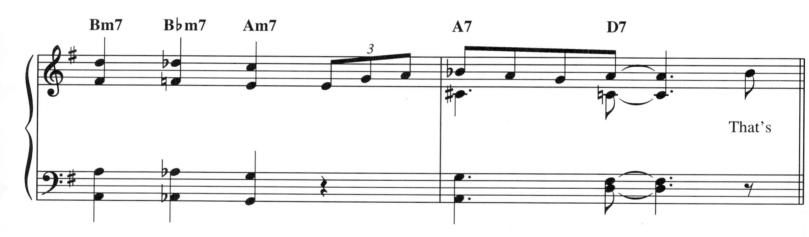

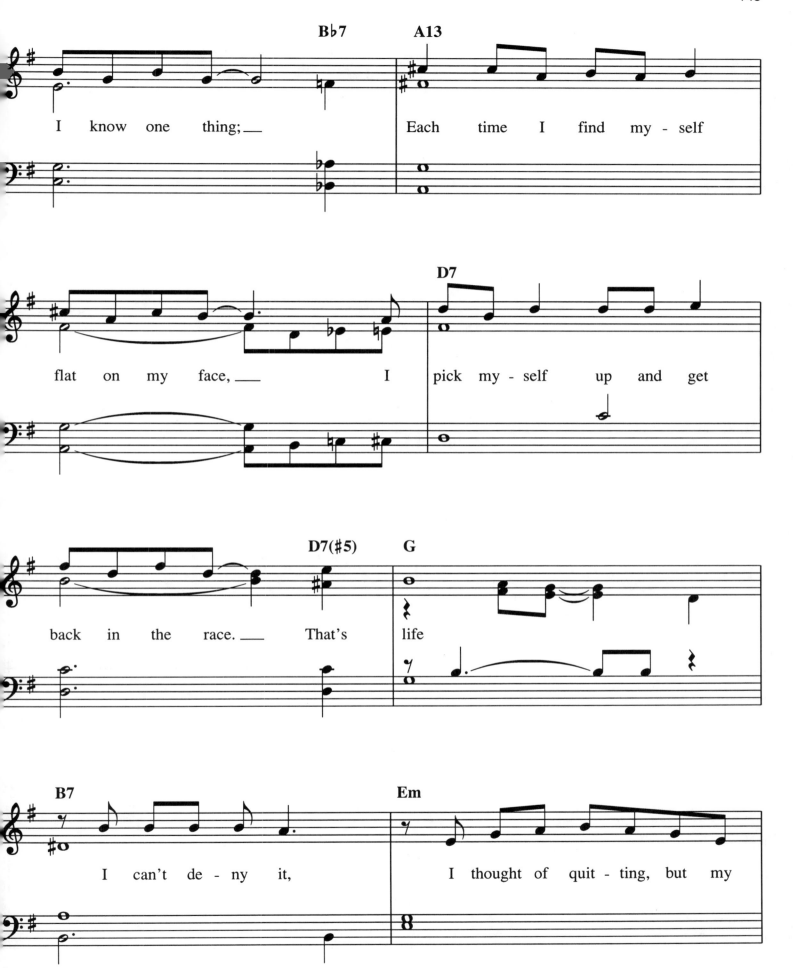

146

WHAT THE WORLD NEEDS NOW IS LOVE

Lyric by HAL DAVID
Music by BURT BACHARACH

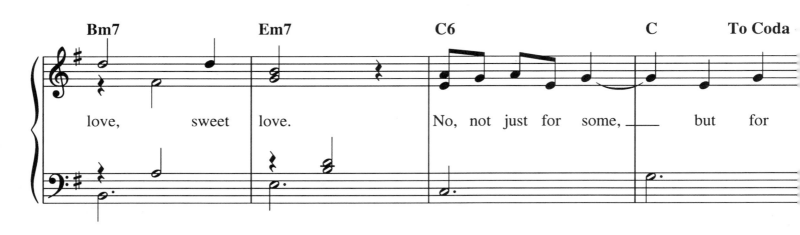

love, sweet love. No, not just for some,___ but for

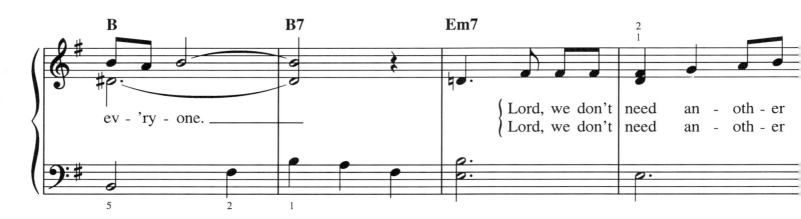

ev - 'ry - one. ___

Lord, we don't need an - oth - er
Lord, we don't need an - oth - er

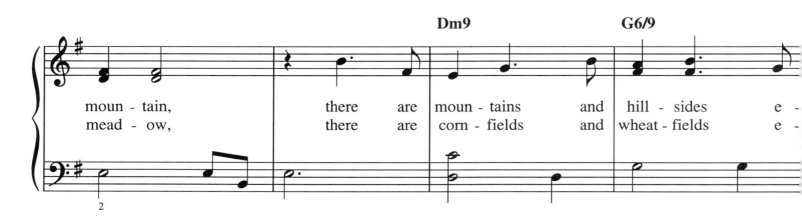

moun - tain, there are moun - tains and hill - sides e -
mead - ow, there are corn - fields and wheat - fields e -

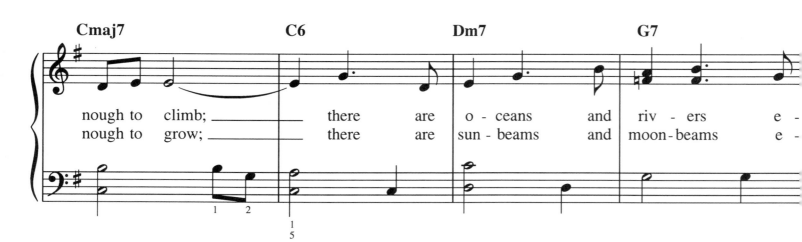

nough to climb; ___ there are o - ceans and riv - ers e -
nough to grow; ___ there are sun - beams and moon - beams e -

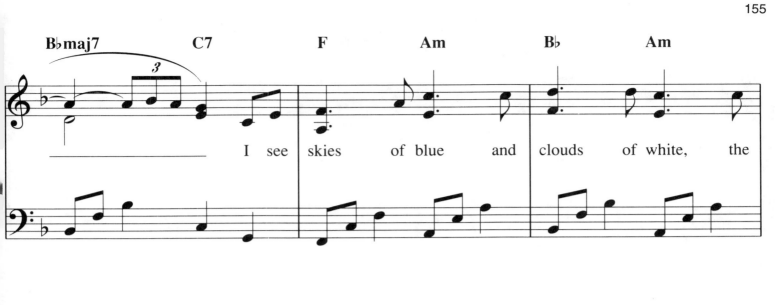

I see skies of blue and clouds of white, the

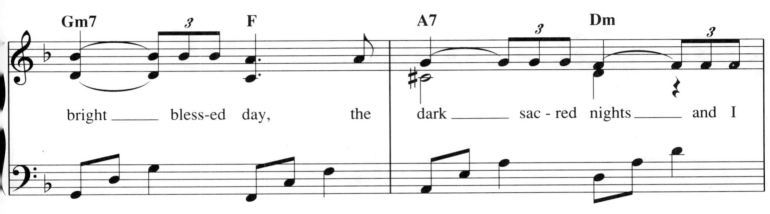

bright _____ bless-ed day, the dark _____ sac - red nights _____ and I

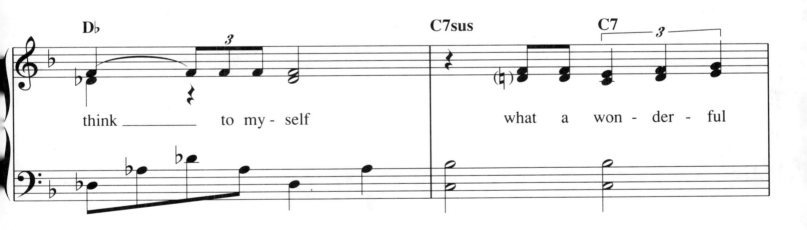

think _____ to my - self what a won - der - ful

world. _____ The col-ors of the rain-bow, so

YOU'RE NOBODY
'TIL SOMEBODY LOVES YOU

Words and Music by RUSS MORGAN,
LARRY STOCK and JAMES CAVANAUGH

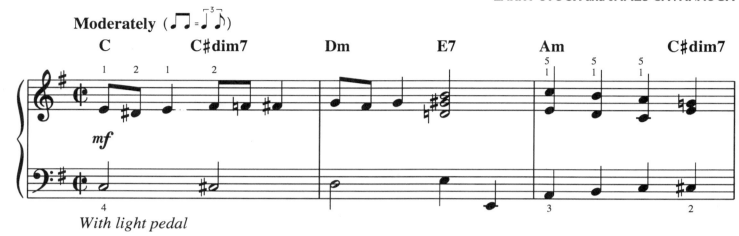

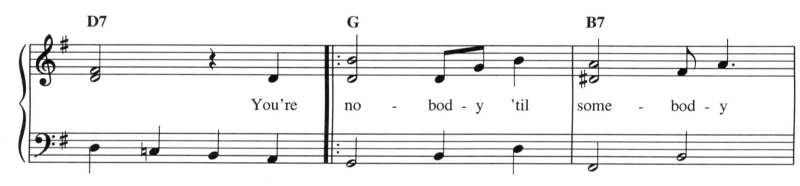

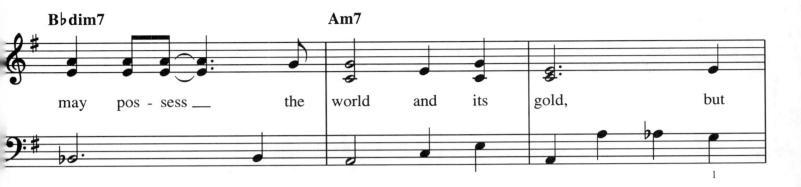

B♭dim7   **Am7**

may pos - sess __ the world and its gold, but

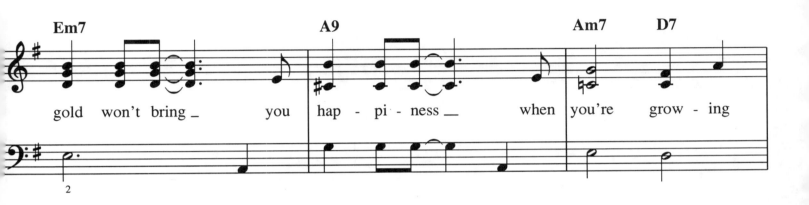

Em7   **A9**   **Am7** **D7**

gold won't bring __ you hap - pi - ness __ when you're grow - ing

G   **B7**

old. The world still is the same, you'll nev - er

E7   **Am**   **E7**

change it. ___ As sure as the stars shine a -

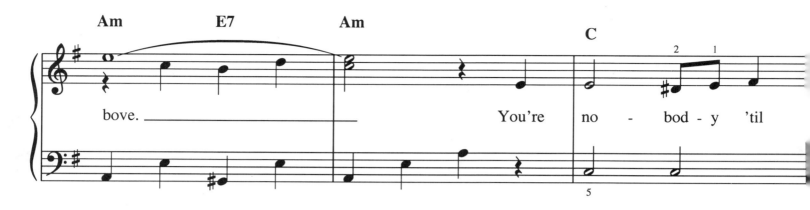

Am **E7** **Am** **C**

bove. _____ You're no - bod - y 'til

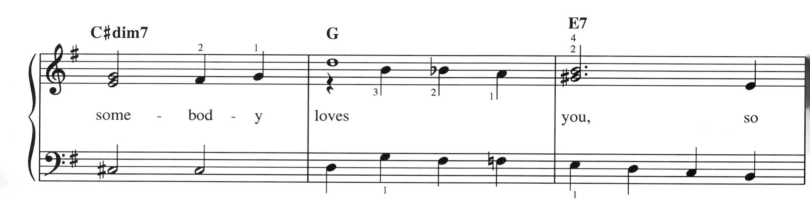

C#dim7 **G** **E7**

some - bod - y loves you, so

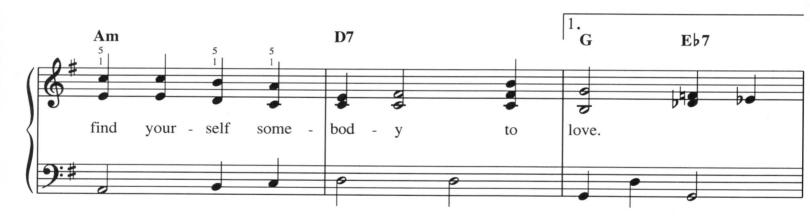

Am **D7** **1. G** **E♭7**

find your - self some - bod - y to love.

D7 **2. G** **E♭7** **D7** **G**

You're love. *rit.*